A Minnnesota Mom

In the Land of the Ancient Mother

VOLUME I
Beginnings

PATRICIA CARLSON STENDAL

Printed in Colombia
By Ransom Press International
Addresses are in back pages of book

Library of Congress Cataloging in Publication Data

Stendal, Patricia C. 1930-

A Minnesota Mom in the Land of the Ancient Mother
Volume I: Beginnings – Long Ago and Far Away

1. Colombia – Kogi Tribe 2. Colombia – 1930's and 1940's. 3. Colombia
   – History
4. Colombia – Missionary. 5. Minnesota – 1920's 6. Norway – 1890's
   7. Murder – Suicide 8. Romance 9. Primitive living. 10. Cultural
   lifestyles.

ISBN 0931221-54-4

Acknowledgements

I want to take this opportunity to thank all who have made this book possible. A special thanks to Ruth Ann Irwin who edited, proofed, and gave valuable input on the entire manuscript of which this is only the first volume. We hope to publish further volumes at the rate of at least one per year. I want to thank my husband, Chad, for living this adventure with me and also my other family members, especially my daughter, Sharon, her husband, Bob, and granddaughters, Lisa and Alethia, for their encouragement along the way in the writing of these books.

I also want to thank Martha Jaramillo for using her talent in page design and Osvaldo Lara, who employed his talent as a graphic artist, to produce the cover, and fix old fotos.

In my mind I have compared the producing of a book to giving birth to a baby. A lot of work and waiting are involved, and towards the end the labor greatly intensifies. Many small agonies must be endured before the finished product, book or baby, is in ones hands or arms. As I have been the author/mother of this project, my daughter, Gloria, has been the midwife. Most of the special touches – selection and placement of pictures and maps have been due to her skill and diligence.

Thanks so much to all of you.

Dedication

To Gloria

Who has been an integral part of this story.

First as a small, handicapped baby,
Then as a helpful child and teenager,
Now, as an adult who literally sees the
Kogis as her brothers and sisters.

It was through your birth that we learned about this tribe.
You have been there with us through all of these experiences.
You have been my sounding board and my confidante.
Your strength of character and wise counsel has kept me
going when I wanted to quit.

God Bless You!

Table of Contents

Volume I
Beginnings Long Ago and Far Away... 11

Stendal Family 1964.

Forward

A few words of explanation about the title: I am not a super mom in any sense of the word. I was just a Minnesota Mom, maybe a little below average in organization and housekeeping skills, when the Lord called us to Colombia, South America. I have been a weak and often reluctant vessel through whom the Lord has chosen to work. I do not wish to take personal credit for the marvelous happenings told in this and the subsequent volumes. (My early life and call to missions is detailed in the forthcoming Volume 2 subtitled *"A Vision is Formed"*).

The term, "Ancient Mother", refers to the name given to the goddess whom the Kogis look to as creator and owner, together with her lesser sons and daughters, who are the spirits of the unique area, the Sierra Nevada de Santa Marta, the highest rising coastal range in the world. These spirits hold the inhabitants of these mountains in a strangle hold. Since 1980 a new element, the Marxist guerrillas have entered the area, followed closely by their enemies, the right wing auto defense groups, the paramilitary. This has caused havoc in the region.

During our first week in Colombia in 1964, we visited a national park in the city of Bogotá. One of the attractions was a relief map of Colombia laid out to a large scale on the ground. In this very mountainous country, one formation attracted our attention, a huge mass of mountain arising on the north coast, right on the edge of the Caribbean Sea. As we new missionaries stood staring at this phenomena, my husband, Chad remarked, "If I were Caleb, I would say, 'Give me this mountain!'" Little did we know that some 17 months later, we would be climbing the lower realms of this mountain area to contact the "little people", the Kogi Indians and that God would make an opening, a miraculous opening, for our family to live among them.

Chadwick M. Stendal

Chad said in 1964, »Give me this mountain!».
Now in the present, like Caleb his eyes have not dimmed,
and the seeds planted so long ago are beginning
to sprout into a strong Christian presence.

Sierra Nevada de Santa Marta, taken at the Parque Jaime
Duque in Bogotá. Water is Caribbean Sea and grass is
Venezuela. River in foreground is the Rio Magdalena,
with Barranquilla at its mouth.
Note that Santa Marta is at the very foot of the mountain.

Mark 4 : 39-41
And he arose, and rebuked the wind,
and said unto the sea, Peace, be still.
And the wind ceased, and there was a great calm.
And he said unto them, Why are ye so fearful?
how is it that ye have no faith?
And they feared exceedingly,
and said one to another,
What manner of man is this,
that even the wind and the sea obey him?

Jesus - Lord of the Sea

Volume I

Beginnings
Long Ago and Far Away

"In the beginning God created the heavens and the earth. The earth was without form and void, and darkness was upon the face of the deep; and the Spirit of God was moving over the face of the waters."

Genesis 1:1

"In the beginning was the Word, and the word was with God, and the Word was God. He was in the begining with God; all things were made by Him, and without Him was not anything made that was made. In Him was life, and the life was the light of men. The light shines in the darkness, and the darkness has not overcome it."

John 1:1-5

"In the beginning was the sea. All was dark; there was no sun, nor moon, nor people, nor animals, nor plants. The sea was everywhere. The sea was the mother. The mother was not like a human nor anything else. She was the spirit of that which was to come, and she was a thought and a memory.

Kogi Myth

Above:
Chaddy, age 10 &
Alfonso, age 17.

Below:
Chaddy cooks
his lunch.

Chapter 1

Stranded in a
Dangerous Village

Santa Marta, Colombia
    January 1968

I couldn't believe my ears! My young son was stranded in an unfamiliar village of primitive Indians, a people noted for their poisonings.

I was lying helplessly in a dingy waterfront hotel room, enduring a nauseating headache, the aftermath of a severe attack of malaria that had hit me without warning the day before. Outside the second story window, a golden sun was sliding into the sea, Billowing clouds filled the horizon with glorious shades of violet and coral. The intense tropical heat of the day was gently giving way. The breeze from the sea had stilled, and the water of the Caribbean looked dark and full of purple shadows; gentle waves lapped at the sandy shore. But the beauty of the enchanting harbor of Santa Marta was lost to me that January afternoon. I lay weakly on a faded green sofa and through the blasting pain in my head tried to comprehend the meaning of the words my husband, Chad, had just spoken to me.

Was it only that morning I had waved good-by to sandy-haired, freckle-nosed Chaddy? He had left with Ron McIntosh, whose blond, boyish appearance belied his proficiency as a jungle pilot, and Alfonso, a Kogi Indian half a head taller than Chaddy, dressed in his typical white homespun garment, his long, black, hair falling loosely over his shoulders. The three had gaily boarded a taxi that would take them some fifteen miles to a small airstrip used by crop-dusting planes at the foot of the mountains. This would be their take-off point for flights into the Kogi village of Mamarongo deep in the mountains.

Chaddy had flashed me a happy smile as I waved to him from the window of the hotel. He was delighted to be off on an adventure, and I was thankful to be able to rest my throbbing head on the pillow again and close my aching eyes against the brightness of the tropical sun.

This was our first chance to live in a Kogi village. Previous attempts on the part of others had failed, and we had waited for this opportunity for years. The Kogi culture is leary of strangers. Their usual greeting to strangers is, *Mitsa neikalika sha?* (When are you leaving?). The Kogis had never allowed outsiders to live among them. True, we had received permission from the head *mama* (chief), but did the villagers, long accustomed to resist outside influences, agree with his decision? We knew that warnings had been sent to *Mama Nacio* from other Kogi villages forbidding him to accept us, and even within the village of *Mamarongo* itself there was strong resistance to our coming.

My malaria attack had come at a most inopportune moment. The short-field airplane of the Jungle Aviation and Radio Service, better known as JAARS, flew on a tight time schedule. By the time we notified them of my unexpected illness, the little airplane had already taken off from its home base at Lomalinda, deep in the eastern plains country of Colombia, and was winging its way through the hazy air of the upper Magdalena Valley. It could not turn back. When

Ron arrived in Santa Marta and learned of my illness, he had decided to make two shuttle flights to transport the others and the gear, leaving me and little Gloria for an additional shuttle flight the next day. That would give me one more day to recuperate before facing the task of organizing a home in the mud house that we hoped had been built for us. Chaddy, Alfonso, the two-way radio for communication with Lomalinda, the shotgun, and some canned food had been selected for the first flight.

After an uneventful landing on the tiny airstrip at *Mamarongo,* Ron carried the radio to the half-finished house that the Indians were building for us near the airstrip and connected it up. Only one Kogi man, *Mama Nacio's* son- in-law Jose Gabriel, was visible. With the boys' help, Ron un- loaded the plane, and after assuring them that he would be right back with Chad and more supplies and household goods, he climbed into the plane, revved up the engine, and took off downhill on the tiny strip. The little plane soon became a speck far in the distance as it flew down the valley between the steep mountainsides.

However to Ron's dismay, he noted a serious problem with the airplane's radio. JAARS regulations would not allow him to fly into the mountains without radio communication, and he was forced to fly straight to Barranquilla, the nearest city in the area where he could have it repaired. Ron had just telephoned our hotel from the airport in Barranquilla. The repair job would take about four days, he said, and there was nothing that could be done except wait for the repair to be finished.

Darkness had fallen over the city of Santa Marta. Small harbor lights twinkled along the beach, around the shipyards along the shoreline to the right, and from several ships lying at anchor in the harbor. Yellow, white, and red, they twinkled like friendly stars against the backdrop of blackness. From the island in the entrance to the harbor, a lighthouse beacon pierced the darkness with its rotating light. Rhythmic waves sounded against the beach as the tide rolled in.

Dust swirled down the narrow, darkened streets of the city, joining with bits of paper in a whirling dance on the street corners, and doors slammed as the wind reversed itself and started blowing stiffly from the mountains to the Caribbean Sea. Nearby, families carried chairs out onto the sidewalks and relaxed in the comparative freshness of the early evening, conversing with neighbors or one another before retiring to their stuffy, windowless bedrooms where droning fans would make possible the rest that they needed to face another stifling day. Tall, stately palm trees swayed in the wind, shapely, graceful forms like shadowy dancers along the sea.

But as I watched from the second floor window, my heart was heavy. What was happening to my son right now? What would a ten-year-old do should the Indians turn hostile? True, Alfonso was with him, but Alfonso too was a stranger in Mamarongo. His home was many days' journey away through the mountains. Alfonso may also be in danger because of his friendship with us, I thought.

What would the boys eat? How would they cook? Would they be worried when the airplane did not return? Would they think there had been a crash? I could do nothing to help them, it seemed. But there was one thing I could do. I committed them both to our Heavenly Father, asking His help and protection. Then I joined Chad and Gloria, who were already asleep.

By the next morning my headache had subsided and had been replaced by a numbing weakness. I still could not tolerate food. Three-year-old Gloria and I went in search of the tamarind juice that a missionary friend had recommended for malaria. We found it at a waterfront cafe a few blocks from our hotel. Sitting at a little outdoor table overlooking the scenic harbor, my thoughts turned to the history of Colombia. In the year 1525 A.D., the Spanish sailed into this same beautiful harbor in quest of gold. Watching a dark, stubby tanker, which lay at anchor taking on oil, I mentally contrasted its ugly form with the stately, graceful sailing vessels I had seen in the history books. They must have made a lovely picture floating on the sparkling, blue Caribbean, sheltered in the cove of the harbor. A huge rock protruded out of the water, forming a small island like a sentinel at the harbor entrance, and the graceful concave arch of the white, sandy beach invited small boats and bathers into its warm shallow waters. The midmorning sun sparkled on the shimmering water, giving a jewel-like quality to the entire scene.

But sadly the cargo carried by the graceful schooners to the New World brought only harm to its indigenous inhabitants. The newcomers were mainly Spanish *hidalgos,* younger sons of wealthy, cultured families who had no inheritance, but whose background and sense of personal importance made them feel they were above common employment or modest business ventures. They were accustomed to spending their days in the public places of Spain, discussing the latest event in the articulate, educated Spanish learned in their childhood, while their own wives and children eked out an existence in direst poverty, taking in washing, or vending wares in the market place. It was to this class of men that the adventure of seeking gold in the New World appealed. This was an enterprise they considered worthy of their participation.

The ships had also brought horses, swords, seeds and farming tools. Since the *hidalgos* were not inclined to do the manual labor themselves, they quickly overpowered the local Indian tribes from whom they extracted forced labor. But the Indians of the northern coast of Colombia were only a step above the *hidalgos* themselves in their disdain for manual labor. They worshipped the *Madre de Antigua* (Ancient Mother), a goddess who, according to their tradition, had arisen out of the Caribbean Sea and created the Indians. She had commissioned them with the task of maintaining the rhythm of nature, bringing the sun up each morning, and bringing in the three-month dry season. To them she had entrusted the secret of life itself, the sprouting of seeds and all fertility.

Since the land and all the objects of nature were possessed by spirit owners, woe to the man who used them without securing proper permission. The Indians had fled from their oppressors whenever possible and escaped to the upper heights of the mountains. Even there they were not safe as the Spaniards, driven by the fever for gold, scaled the heights, massacring all those whom they encountered in their frantic search for riches. After leaving the villages in shambles and putting the heads of the murdered *mamas* on poles along the trails as warnings to any who thought to oppose them, the main gold search moved down the Magdalena River to the central plateau of Bogotá between two ranges of the Andes Mountains.

Gloria's small voice interrupted my reverie, "Will Chaddy be all right? The Kogis won't poison him, will they, Mama? Won't Alfonso take care of him?" Of her three older siblings, fun-loving Chaddy was her favorite.

"I hope he will, honey," I responded, finishing my juice. "We will trust God to take care of him."

We walked slowly along the waterfront, passing the fashionable Pan-American Hotel. How I enjoyed the few occasions when we had eaten dinner in there, but now we had to watch our pesos. On sudden inspiration we went in, and I purchased several slices of pineapple pie to take back to our hotel, enjoying the brief moments of air- conditioned comfort. This was the only place in Santa Marta that boasted air-conditioning and American style pastries.

Back at our dingy hotel I found Hugh and Marty Tracy, a young newly married couple who were going to work with the neighboring tribe, the Arhuacos, sipping tall glasses of iced Colombian coffee. "Good news!" they greeted us, "Chaddy is all right!"

Chad had put through a telephone call to the mission headquarters in Bogotá. They had picked up their two-way radio and contacted the operator at the base in Lomalinda. "Chaddy is fine," they were told. "He has called in four times this morning. He likes to talk on the radio."

The next Monday we were all flown to Mamarongo. We found out that upon their arrival, Chaddy and Alfonso had taken the shotgun and killed game birds. These were presented as a gift to the nearest Kogi family, and after that the boys were always welcome at at that house at mealtime. In the daytime Chaddy entered into the daily work of the Kogi men, which happened to be clearing the land to be planted at the start of the rainy season. Evenings, the boys entertained the Kogis by making a racetrack in the dirt floor of our new house and racing small battery-operated cars with flashing lights.

By the time the rest of us had arrived, Chaddy had broken the ice and made friends with the people of Mamarongo. "We like Chaddy," one man told us. "He is a Kogi."

Stendal Family arriving with airplane.

An artist's rendition of the Sierra Nevada de Santa Marta from sea level drawn by my grandson, Kessel Stendal, age 12.

Chapter 2

The Majestic Giant

Mamarongo in the Sierra Nevada of Santa Marta
  March 1968

Standing like a rocky fortress, its base in the humid
tropical lowlands, its northern foothills washed by the sparkling blue, foam-kissed breakers of the Caribbean Sea, with
central turrets soaring up some 19,000 feet above the ocean
into the rarefied, frigid atmosphere of the equatorial heights,
the majestic Sierra Nevada of Santa Marta welcomed the
first soft rays of morning light on its eastern slopes. Rising
like a frosted island from the encircling greenery of the lowlands, the Sierra had for centuries serenely guarded its mys-
teries held hidden in secluded valleys enfolded among the
rocky ridges. Secrets at which the inhabitants of the coastal
plains could only wonder and conjecture as from time to time
several of the mysterious inhabitants of the Sierra highlands
made their way into the lowland villages to purchase the few
manufactured items which were desired in their simple way
of life.

To the west lay the fertile valley of the Magdalena River,
that first primitive highway by which Spanish conquerors of

long ago entered the heartland of Colombia, seeking the trea-
sure of *El Dorado* (the Golden One) to the east in the narrow
valley separating the Sierra from the eastern range of the
Andes lay the thriving city of Valledupar; and to the north-
west the arid Guajira peninsula where the matriarchal, goat-
herding Guajiro Indians eked out a livelihood from the desert,
colorful in their loose, flowing garments. To the south were
rolling foothills where the lowlanders had already claimed the
land, leaving its original inhabitants, the Chimila Indians working as serfs with a rage that could not be calmed, and beyond
lay an extensive swampland with brackish, putrid waters.

Although consisting of an area merely eighty miles in di-
ameter, the more than three and a half mile perpendicular
dimension of the fortress-like region prohibited entrance to
all but the most hardy of limb and lungs. On the western
slopes swift, cold rivers, flowing for centuries, had rutted the
topography of the terrain carrying turbulent, icy water from
the snow-capped peaks, cascading over mammoth rocks and
winding torturously, seeking the path of least resistance to
the verdant plains below.

In spite of the difficulty of travel, the lure of the lush, fertile, *tierras templadas* (temperate lands) between 2,500 and
6,000 feet above sea level had attracted colonizers whose
coffee plantations were spreading over the more accessible
lands. Although a few primitive roads had been laboriously
cut into the foothills and switch-backed up the mountainsides
to supply several frontier-style towns in the lower reaches of
the temperate altitudes, the would-be invader must for the
most part depend upon the twisting trails which could only
be traversed by sure-footed mules, broad-backed *bueyes*
(oxen), or well-conditioned humans whose lungs were adapted
to the steep ascents, and whose muscular legs could stand
the pounding of frequent steep drops of thousands of feet.

However above 4,000 feet and a day's travel from the
few towns, the majestic fortress was still in the possession of
its indigenous inhabitants — they who formed the soul of the

tranquil giant, and who looked down upon the invaders and their civilization as being a few inconsequential grasshoppers or playful puppies who dared to frolic around the feet of the placid giant, a nuisance to be sure, but of no real significance, to be utilized for some service occasionally, but whose existence had little importance to the basic and important issues of life and nature.

As the warm shafts of light crept up and over the pinnacles of the lofty summits of the center of the citadel and started to penetrate the chilly, damp darkness of the western hollow on the humid, windward side of the mountains, a lone figure could be seen moving swiftly over a small winding trail leading to a most unusual geographic formation in this rugged terrain. Two rivers coming together in a 'V,' the mighty Tucarinca and the slightly smaller River of Mamarongo — swift, icy, turbulent mountain streams — had somehow protected and allowed to form a long, narrow strip of level land. Cleared of trees long ago for use as a pasture, it now had recently been freed of rocks, and its grassy surface bore an uncanny resemblance to a tiny airstrip. At its southern tip and off to one side, stood several simple habitations whose circular walls of strips of woven wild cane and peaked, thatched roofs manifested the unmistakable handiwork of the Kogi Indians, the native inhabitants of this isolated region.

But stranger still, midway up the rudimentary airstrip and off to the right stood a rectangular house of mud construction with an aluminum roof, which gleamed in the early morning light. The sheets of roofing had been rather inexpertly pieced together, giving a somewhat patchwork appearance but adequately protecting the occupants from the torrential downpours which fell around noon most days as the warm, moisture laden air of the Caribbean coast was carried by the prevailing daytime wind currents and met the high, cold atmosphere of the upper altitudes. The fragrant aroma of freshly brewed coffee, and the wisps of smoke emanating from the ventilation space in the upper wall under the roof indicated that inside someone was preparing breakfast over a wood fire. It was to this strange habitation that the small, lone figure hurried.

Inside the crude dwelling, I was just sprinkling dry oatmeal into an aluminum kettle suspended over the fire, thankful for the warmth from the blaze as I shivered in the chilly morning dampness when *Manijildu* appeared in the doorway. To the uninitiated, he would have seemed a startling figure with his long, uncombed black hair, homespun, soiled white clothing, and diminutive, childlike body; but I was now growing accustomed to this distinctive tribe. I knew at once that he had come for me. I was ready to go with him. The family breakfast was ready. Powdered milk was already mixed in a plastic pitcher on the table, and the oatmeal and coffee had been prepared.

A cup of *tinto* (strong, black Colombian coffee) occupied *Manihildu* while I grabbed my *gama* (Indian carrying bag made of jute fibers, known best as the material from which gunny sacks are made) and bade my husband and children good-by. How glad I was that the bag was packed and ready. The nervous butterflies that I could already feel starting in my stomach would not have allowed for calm, careful selection of medicines this morning.

"You better get yourself ready. It looks like they will be asking you for help," Chad had remarked the evening before as we had relaxed for a minute around the kitchen table after the supper dishes were put away. The entire Kogi Indian community of Mamarongo knew that *Manihildu*'s young wife had gone into labor the morning before.

"Is it born yet? Is it born yet?" the Kogis asked each other throughout the day.

Kogi mothers had been known to experience trouble in childbirth. These pygmy-like people, stunted by the low protein banana diet during their growing years, sometimes cannot deliver the baby who becomes normal sized, absorbing whatever nutrition is available, leaving less for the mother's body. We had been told of a woman who not long before had begged to be cut open in a desperate attempt to deliver a baby that was too large to fit through the birth canal. Her request had been granted with an unsterile *machete* (long, jungle knife), but both mother and child had died.

However realizing that first-born babies often take some time in arriving, I had not been too concerned yesterday, nevertheless I was burning with curiosity to know something of Kogi birth customs and so offered my services when the husband had dropped by in the afternoon for a cup of *tinto*.

The Kogis, having suffered the indignity of invasion by the early European gold-seekers with their atrocities and utter disregard for Indian life and culture, had retreated up into their mountain fortress and reformed their culture, weaving into it rigid safeguards which would protect them from the intrusion of the outside world. Even after four centuries, the Kogis had not forgotten. Each individual at puberty vows fidelity to his customs, religion and language and pledges to guard them from intruders. In fact at this time, 1968, a Kogi who was considered to be too friendly with outsiders risked having poison slipped into his food. The presence of our family in the Kogi village of Mamarongo was a miracle and followed more than two years of effort.

"I will let you know if I need you," *Manihildu* had curtly informed me yesterday after my offer of assistance. Was not his old mother, Marta, the expert midwife of the area? His mother-in-law also was very experienced in attending Kogi mothers. It had been most unlikely that any help would be needed, but now, this morning, he had showed up asking for my help.

My formal training had been in the field of education, but since my arrival in the Kogi tribe, of necessity I had spent far more time in medical treatment than in teaching. It seemed that our first obligation was to keep the people alive until we could learn their language and teach them to read.

When nightfall had brought no announcement of the birth, I went ahead and prepared my *gama* (carrying bag) by Coleman lantern light. A few analgesics which might help the pain of childbirth, several disposable hypodermic syringes with their needles, cotton, alcohol, a small rubber syringe to clear the baby's airway if necessary, urgotrate pills in case of hemorrhage, dressings for the umbilical cord, and a white bath towel to provide a clean working surface. What more could I take? I did not know. Although I was the mother of four children, my western culture had effectively insulated me from the practicalities of childbirth.

Now as I plodded along the narrow trail behind my Indian guide, my mind was racing. I scarcely noticed the small biting gnats that were feasting on my bare legs above my ankle

Pat on the trail.

socks. I took stock of my scant training and experience in obstetrics. When my husband and I had been missionary trainees in southern Mexico, the Jungle Camp doctor had lectured us on basic birth procedures, however the one previous occasion when I had been asked to attend a woman in childbirth, I had found myself ill prepared. Although the woman and her child came through the experience just fine, her farmer husband had been more helpful than I was.

Trudging along the trail behind *Manihildu*, one phrase from the lecture at Jungle Camp kept reoccurring in my mind. "In an Indian tribe," the missionary doctor had said, "It is unlikely that you will be called for a normal delivery. The Indians themselves are well able to handle these. You will be called in to attend abnormal presentations and other life threatening situations, such as hemorrhage, which a person with your limited training and equipment is unable to handle." He then proceeded to demonstrate with a rubber doll a few techniques of assisting babies who were making their entrance into the world in some position other than the usual.

As we passed a cleared area, I consciously focused my attention on the young coffee trees growing on both sides of the trail. My husband had encouraged their planting, and in time they would produce tiny, round, green balls that would ripen into red cherry-like berries — the famous Colombian mountain grown coffee — which we hoped would provide needed cash income for the Kogi economy to enable them to purchase the few things like cooking pots and blankets that they liked. Tall, swaying *platano* (plantain) trees gently waved their large, dew covered leaves in the cool morning breeze, shading the delicate coffee plants and giving promise of the hearty cooking bananas which are the mainstay of Kogi nutrition.

Up and over a knoll the trail went. Then into the tangled jungle where long hanging vines trailed from towering laurel trees whose high-canopied branches obscured the rising rays of morning sun. Down, down, down we plunged; my feet selecting the spots just vacated by the bare, swift feet ahead of me — over fallen logs, stooping under partially fallen trees, jumping from rock to rock over the low, muddy parts of the trail. As my eyes took in the breathtaking beauty of God's creation, I realized that I was actually enjoying this escape from my mud-walled kitchen, uncertain though I was about what would await me at *Manihildu's* house.

All of a sudden I remembered something! In my haste to accompany *Manihildu*, I had forgotten to secure permission from our Kogi guard. Although we had been allowed to live in the Kogi village, a machete-armed sentinel maintained a close watch on our activities and challenged us should we attempt to leave the immediate area of our house and airstrip. A house call to a sick Kogi was our only opportunity to venture into the magnificent rain forests of the area. The present generation had not forgotten the indignities of the past and was taking no chance with foreigners.

But the urgency of my guide reminded me that this was not a pleasure excursion. Undoubtedly the situation awaiting me was one of the life threatening ones the doctor had mentioned. How could I expect to do anything to help? Once again I reviewed in my mind my qualifications: the Jungle Camp class, my experiences as a woman and as a mother, the embarrassing inadequacy in my attempt to help the colonist woman, and some extracurricular reading in the medical books we had acquired. Yet, there was one asset left. On this I must pin all hope for the suffering human sister to whose aid my feet were so rapidly carrying me. My heart was now pounding, not only with the physical exertion of the mountain trail. Would I, reserved, undistinguished Minnesota Mom that I was, be able to be a catalyst that would bring the healing, miracle working power of Almighty God to the aid of this agonizing Kogi creature? There was no way to call in a request to my church, my pastor nor the ladies in my prayer group. It was up to God, as He might choose to manifest Himself through me.

Manihildu and his wife, whom Pat assisted in a difficult childbirth.

Chapter 3

A Mysterious Birth

Manihildu further quickened his pace. His long, un-cut black hair swayed below a brown fedora type hat. A *machete* (long, sharp jungle knife) supported from his head by a narrow leather strap, glistened in the sun, which was now peering over the crest of the mountains to the east. The small, lithe body clad in loosely fitting hand woven garments gave the impression of child likeness; yet he was a mature man in his mid thirties. This was not his first wife, yet I knew that he had no living children.

Manihildu's brother, Jose Gabriel, had built our house and invited us to live on his land in spite of the uneasiness of some of his neighbors. One day Jose had explained to me the reason for his invitation. He told me of a former wife and three children who had all died in an epidemic, leaving him alone. Now he had taken a new wife and started another family. "I want you and Chad near me, " he confessed, "So that I might have at least one child who survives me." Kogi infant mortality was very high.

As I hurried along the trail, my heart was crying out to God, outstripping even the rapid pace of my feet. "Oh, Lord! Spare this woman!" I inwardly cried. "Help me to know what to do for her and her baby. I know my inadequacy! Undertake by your Spirit for my lacks! Manifest Your great power! Bring glory to Your name! I yield myself into Your hands as Your instrument to minister to this girl."

When I could think of nothing else to say, I continued in an attitude of prayer, allowing my heart to reach out to my loving heavenly Father in words only intelligible to His ears. I felt at peace. The quiet confidence of the Lord's presence filled my being. We were now on the last descent. I could see the grouping of three little thatched-roofed buildings in the bare, fenced clearing — for once in a low, flat glen instead of on the crest of a lofty hill.

Kogi farms have 2 huts. The larger one is for the men and the smaller one is for the women and young children.

As we approached the buildings, a low, guttural sound from Manihildu brought two elderly women into the center of the clearing. Their wrinkled, brown faces showed the strain of the long hours of struggle. They both wore the usual ingenious wrap-around garments used by adult Kogi women, each one made of a single piece of white cotton material. By a complex system of ties, the one-piece rectangular cloth becomes a sarong-like dress, leaving one shoulder bare. The length was adjusted by a belt at the waist, the extra material bunched up around the middle of the body during the day and loosened to let the skirt cover the legs at night. Several strands of plum colored beads hung from the neck of one woman. The neck of the older one was completely bare, very different from the younger Kogi women whose many heavy coils of colorful beads are their pride and security. I wondered where they had the laboring girl. I knew that one of the buildings would be the men's house where no woman, myself included, may enter.

The grim expressions and despairing droop of the shoulders of the aged women indicated that the situation had not improved. After a few more exchanges with the women, Manihildu led me to the smallest and most dilapidated of the three buildings. As we approached I saw that it was the coop where the chickens are secured at night against marauding foxes and jaguars. This was unreal! Was the poor girl in there?

But no, he was leading me around the chicken coop. It was very dark there in the shadows. Green and gray mosses reveled in the dank dampness, giving off their pungent odors. Small black insects scurried around, and disturbed brown spiders indicated displeasure at the invasion of their environment. "In there," he indicated. He was motioning me to a small area between the back of the chicken coop and a crude wooden fence, which separated the clearing from the surrounding jungle.

As my eyes became accustomed to the darkness, I saw my patient. She was lying in the middle of the space in the darkest part, wedged in tightly between the coop and the fence. I could not imagine why she was there, but by now I was becoming accustomed to strange Kogi customs. There were many things in the language and culture, which did not seem reasonable to my western way of thinking. I had come to help this woman, and I was determined to do my best. I knew that back at our house at the side of the airstrip, Chad and the children were praying. I also gained strength from the knowledge that many of our friends in the United States were praying for us and the Kogi tribe every day. I decided to proceed in faith to do all that I could for her.

Her pain was my first concern. (Back in the '50's and '60's, we Americans were not so much into natural childbirth methods but were focused on pain relief.) Going around the house, ignoring the slimy moss and squirmy insects, I dropped to my knees and crawled in so that I could get near her mouth. I spooned in the correct dosage of the liquid analgesic I had chosen the night before. Then I crawled out, laid my white towel out on the ground in the sunlight and began to prepare an injection. Tucking my full skirt around me, I crawled back in, gave the injection in the arm, then crawled out, ran around the chicken coop again and crawled in from the other side to see if I could examine her abdomen and possibly determine the position of the baby. Meanwhile the two women and Manihildu observed all my activities silently and soberly, no doubt commenting that the North American woman had very strange customs.

The young woman looked very glad to see me and submitted patiently to my inexpert, probing fingers. I made no attempt to disrobe her for the examination, as her garment was far too complicated for me to undo, and I was much too unsure of myself. The labor was far advanced. The water had broken long before, and I could feel the baby's tiny form very easily. It was a breech presentation. The hard, round head was still high in the mother's abdomen.

My heart sank. I knew what this meant. My youngest child, Gloria, had also been a breech. After unsuccessful attempts to change her position, she had been delivered feet first. I had been anesthetized in the clinic in Bogotá, Colombia's capital city, but I knew that the doctor and Miss Annie, the maternity nurse, had managed to deliver her by manipulating her by the feet. I also knew that both of our lives had been in grave danger at several points during the delivery.

I was horrified to think that I might have to reach into this woman's body in this contaminated place without even the protection of a sterile glove, yet except for the chance of birthplace, I could have been the one experiencing the grinding pains of childbirth in a little mud hut with only the help of an unsanitary, ill-trained midwife.

Vaguely I remembered the Jungle Camp doctor's demonstration with the rubber doll. I crawled out from behind the chicken coop and attempted to communicate with Manihildu using my limited Kogi and his limited Spanish. I attempted to tell him that the baby was coming feet first instead of head first; that I was not very experienced in this, but that with his permission I would be willing to try to get a hold on the feet and manipulate the baby out.

While I was explaining this, suddenly the girl came crawling out from behind the chicken coop. Staggering unsteadily between the two old women who rushed to support her, she entered the women's house and collapsed on top of some indescribably filthy rags, which had been ground into the dirt of the earthen floor. Immediately she fell into a deep sleep. The two older women disappeared, and I was still trying to explain the situation to Manihildu as we entered the house.

"No! No! No!" he exclaimed when he understood what I was proposing. Then he too disappeared.

I did not know what to do. Never have I felt more helpless. I sat down on a low, concave bench carved from a tree stump. I was emotionally exhausted. At least the girl was not suffering at the moment, but she had been in labor now for more than twenty-four hours. If she could not give birth to this baby, it was certain death for the two of them. It would take days to carry her over these rugged mountain trails to the nearest medical aid, and it was doubtful if the Kogis would actually attempt to do it. Death in childbirth was a common enough fate for Kogi women. The husband had not encouraged any heroic intervention on my part. Had they all gone off and left me to witness her death alone? A common expression came to mind: When all else fails, pray. Pray, I did! With all my heart! As I sat on that crude, low stool, the only piece of furniture in the darkened hut, with the exhausted woman stretched out on her filthy rags, I again felt the peace and presence of God. I knew that I could not save this woman, but she was in God's hands.

The two elderly women reappeared, and before my amazed eyes, without disturbing the extended cloth garment which covered the girl from her chest to her ankles, they turned that baby around, just as neatly as could be. Working slowly and expertly, their four hands moving as if coordinated and synchronized, they turned that tiny form within its mother's body. For a bit it lay transverse, then I saw them start to make headway in forcing the head down. Two hands always maintained the position gained while the other two were coaxing the diminutive parts into the more favorable position. The patient was still asleep. I continued praying, but with my eyes wide open.

At last the turn was completed. One woman pushed the head firmly into the birth canal, and the other raised the mother to an upright squatting position. Another push on the new mother's abdomen by the first woman, and the baby dropped easily into the back of the mother's skirt, which was now drawn tautly by the squatting legs. The mother immediately woke up. The old woman retrieved the baby from the skirt and handed him to the mother who, dazedly maintaining her squatting position, cradled her newborn infant in her arms, the little body still attached by the umbilical cord.

I couldn't believe my eyes. I sat and watched in amazement until my attention was caught by a lot of commotion. There was a lot of running around and shouting. Obviously the Kogis were looking for something. Each of the women and Manihildu thought that someone else should know where it was. At last they found it: a certain sharp reed, which is traditionally used to sever the cord. This custom undoubtedly saves many little Kogi lives from infection that could be caused by contaminated knives or other sharp instruments.

The cord was tied and cut without incident. The placenta was delivered, placed in an old gourd, and given to Manihildu to bury. Water was warmed and splashed on the newborn boy. Then came the time to wrap up the baby. One of the grandmothers reached for the filthy rags on which the mother had been lying. Quickly I extended the white towel.

"Clothes for the baby," I explained. With thanks, they accepted the towel to be the baby's receiving blanket. Next, the mother's dress was changed, still without exposing her body. The clean one was tied and slipped on over the soiled. Then the dirty one was untied and peeled out from underneath. The new mother then collapsed on her rags for a much-needed rest, and the two grandmothers turned to me.

They thanked me profusely, giving me all the credit for the successful birth. Then the elderly Marta, renowned midwife of the Kogi tribe, turned to me and said, "I want you to be at my side when my other daughter-in-law has her baby next month."

I started down the trail for home, marveling at the events I had just witnessed. A number of questions arose in my mind: Why was the girl behind the chicken coop? Why had they called me in the first place? Why hadn't the grandmothers just turned the baby around since they were so expert? Since they handled the birth so expertly, why had they thanked me so extravagantly in a manner so different from the usual stoicism of the Kogis?

I continued to ponder these questions for a long time.

Kogi woman with baby.

Maria Antonia and baby.

Maria Antonia bathes Roberto.

Chapter 4

A New Grandson

Two weeks later while I was still mulling over these matters in my mind, the next call came. Once again I was in the kitchen preparing breakfast. The *gama* hung ready with the same equipment as before. Three-year-old Gloria cried bitterly at being left. She wanted to go with me to see the new baby. She knew that her little playmate, Jose *Nungutse* (Little Jose) was going to have a new baby sister or brother.

In no time I had crossed the airstrip and covered the 100 yards between Jose Gabriel's house and mine. Stooping to enter the small, round hut, I saw Maria Antonia, my nearest neighbor, squatting in the shadows to my left. As the pains gripped her body she threw herself from side to side. "What pain! What pain!" she shrieked.

Old Marta, her mother-in-law, was wringing her hands in anxiety. Her face relaxed as I entered and lit up in a welcoming smile.

"When did the pains start?" I asked Jose Gabriel.

"About an hour ago," was the reply.

Another pain wracked Maria Antonia's body. "Give her the medicine! Give her the medicine!" the husband implored.

I was afraid to give pain medicine so early for fear of retarding and prolonging the labor, so I maneuvered for time.

"First I have to examine her to see if the baby is in the right position," I firmly demanded.

With much insistence, Maria Antonia was persuaded to lie down on her cowhide-sleeping pad to be examined. The cowhide, four cooking kettles of various sizes, a hammock, and several woolen blankets marked Jose Gabriel as one of the more affluent members of the Kogi tribe. Actually the wealth came from Maria Antonia, daughter of the famous *Mama Nacio*, the most powerful of the Kogi shamans on the western side of the mountains. To the Kogi mind, it was he who brought the sun up in the morning and put it down at night. His knowledge and ability to control meteorological conditions by dances and chants brought the dry season once a year so that cleared fields could be burned in preparation for the next planting. Without question he was the most important man, not only in the tribe, but also in the world, according to the thinking of the Kogis on this side of the mountains. Should anything happen to him, it would mean the end of the world as his sons were young, and no one had been trained to take his place. The new life that Maria Antonia was striving to bring to the light of day would carry the bloodline of the Kogi equivalent of royalty.

Checking Maria Antonia's abdomen was far different from the similar examination I had performed on her sister-in-law two weeks before. While the first woman had been thin, the liquid long gone, and each part of the baby easy to feel, Maria Antonia's abdomen was thick and spongy, full of amniotic fluid, and she wouldn't lay still for a minute. Try as I might, I could not define any parts of the baby. As another pain hit her, Maria Antonia jumped from my grasp and resumed her squatting position, screaming and thrashing.

"*Eldimedzhio! Eldimedzhio!* (The medicine, The medicine)," the relatives pleaded. I felt myself almost caught up in their terror and panic. Against my better judgment, I spooned the liquid into her grateful mouth and injected her in the arm.

Assuring them that I would return shortly, I hurried home to see how my family was getting along. I wanted to prevent Gloria from running over to her friend's house to find me. Kogi taboos prevent children, young men, and women who have not yet born children from witnessing childbirth. As I crawled out of the low hut into the bright freshness of the mountain morning, my mind was troubled. Had I been talked into administering the medicine too soon? The Jungle Camp doctor had warned us that pain relievers should not be given until delivery was imminent. One hour into labor did not seem very long, but the pains were very strong and close together. I prayed that I had done no damage.

Returning to our house, I found nine-year-old Mariana playing with Gloria and Little Jose. Her cheery smile and gentle ways made her an excellent baby sitter, and as the oldest of five sisters, she was experienced as well. When my request for a woman to help me was denied by the Mamarongo men's council (Kogi women do not work outside of their own families, they had said), Mariana had come with her father to volunteer her services. Looking at Mariana, I had wondered how she could be of any help at all. She was only a head taller than Gloria. However I soon found that she could bring me water from the stream, peel *platanos and yuca*

Mariana washes the dishes, while carrying her baby sister on her back.

(manioc), keep the fire going, and sweep; but she refused to wash our clothes. In her eyes they were not even dirty yet.

Dishes were a struggle for her. Kogi homes have one cup and one spoon. The men eat first, taking the pieces of *yuca* and *platanos* directly from the kettles. The spoon and the cup are passed around to be shared by all. After the men have finished eating, the kettles and utensils are passed into the house to be used by the women and girls. Our stack of cups, plates, and spoons to be washed in hot soapy water and scalded three times a day seemed like a lot of unnecessary work. However since the most important activity in Mariana's life was mealtime, and the serving of the next meal seemed to depend on getting the dishes washed, she was usually willing to help out. As Jose Gabriel was her maternal uncle, it was culturally acceptable for her to sleep in the house with Maria Antonia and help me in the daytime. As I stacked the dishes and prepared the dishwater for Mariana, my thoughts kept returning to Maria Antonia. How long would her labor last? What would the outcome be?

My earlier experience with Kogi childbirth had strengthened my confidence, not in my skills as a midwife, but in the Lord's power and willingness to intervene. I breathed a silent prayer as I placed the enamelware plates in the round plastic tub and added soap powder and warm water. Maria Antonia was probably resting quietly after taking the medicine; I just hoped that the drugs had not weakened the labor pains too much.

I wanted to stay away longer to give more time for the labor to progress before I returned and was pressured by the Jose Gabriel and his mother to do something more, but I couldn't wait. I was too curious to find out what was happening in the other house. With a gesture to Mariana, I quietly slipped out and ran down the airstrip to Maria Antonia's house.

What a scene met my eyes. "I am still hurting just as badly" she screeched at me accusingly, her eyes adding that my medicine had done no good at all. Her dress was disheveled, most of the ties loosened by her incessant thrashing and bouncing.

Marta was screaming that her daughter-in-law was dying, that the baby was badly positioned just like the other one, and that the medicine had done no good. She was accusing her son, Jose Gabriel, telling him to confess his sins, that undoubtedly it was his fault that this disaster was happening. He just stood there, silent and morose. At last, exhausted by her tirade, Marta grabbed one of the low benches with both hands, bending from the waist head down, her long black hair streaming down upon the wooden bench, she began to pray to her deity, the ancient mother, most likely confessing her own sins, some infraction of tribal taboos.

As my mind recovered from the shock of finding them in such distress, I asked Maria Antonia to lie down to be examined again, but my words went unheeded. She was far too hysterical with pain and fear. Her only thought was to maintain her upright position. Her husband was supporting her now, his hands under her armpits. Marta implored me to do something. Terrified myself, I knelt in front of her to at least see if I could determine the baby's position. As I gently laid my hand on her abdomen, the grandson of Mama Nacio suddenly made his entrance into the world. He landed head first into the taut net formed by the back of his mother's skirt, then with a little bounce shot forward onto a heap of dry leaves that had been piled in just the right spot. It was a climactic moment.

Knowing that many primitive tribes have birth customs giving significance to the picking up of the child, although the tiny form was right in front of me, I hesitated, letting Marta, the grandmother, be the one to touch him first. He was a beautiful baby — plump and with good color. Marta handed him to me, then busied herself by warming water on the smoldering fire, which she then sloshed over the slippery body in my hands. I was glad the Jungle Camp doctor had demonstrated with the rubber doll how to get a good grip on a slimy newborn. The sterile manicure scissors that I pulled out of my *gama* saved the cord from being cut with Jose Gabriel's pocketknife. Evidently he had forgotten to provide the special reed. I was asked for clothes, and soon the little one was cozily enveloped in the white towel.

We were all hilariously happy after the emotional strain of a few minutes before. I was babbling away in my limited Kogi, trying to say that the baby was cute and that I liked him. I inadvertently used a verb with a double meaning. It could mean, I like him, which was what I meant, but it could also be taken, as I want him. To my surprise, Jose Gabriel turned to me and said, "You can have him as soon as he is old enough to leave his mother."

His father named him, Roberto, on the spot, and from that time on, he was considered to belong to me.

Years of further observation, including other Kogi childbirth experiences, have shed some light on the puzzling aspects of these two births. I think the girl had crawled behind the chicken coop to escape from the midwives and lie down. Kogi women are not allowed to lie down during labor. The older women hit them and shame them to keep them in an upright position. They depend heavily on the force of gravity to facilitate the birth.

It is possible that the old women did not know the position of the first woman's baby, or if they did know, she could have been too hysterical to submit to their manipulation. The pain medicine that I administered in both cases was not very strong. The first girl was so worn out that it took effect and relaxed her enough that the turning could be accomplished. On the other hand it had little or no effect on Maria Antonia. Maria Antonia had probably been in the beginning stages of labor all through the night, and it only came to Jose Gabriel's attention in the morning, therefore he said it only started an hour ago. She was obviously in the last part of her labor when I came into the picture.

I found out that babies are often given to a grandmother or grandfather or even another relative at birth. It is not a permanent relinquishing on the part of the parents, but a temporary loaning. The child eventually returns to the parents. When Roberto was two I made it clear to his mother that I would not take him from her, but I would be another grandmother for him and give him special treatment. When he was seven he came out of the tribe with us and was like a brother to Gloria for several years. I taught him to read and write, and he picked up Spanish. Later on he came out again and even went to a Colombian school for a while. Presently he has a wife and family and is somewhat of a leader in the tribe. He still considers me his grandmother. While he has not made a strong stand as a Christian, I believe the Lord is not done with him yet.

One problem remains: A doctor with whom I spoke and an obstetric book which I read both stated that after the amniotic fluid is gone, it is impossible to turn a child within the uterus. I do believe that what I witnessed that day was a miracle wrought by our loving Heavenly Father who sent me and my family from Minneapolis, Minnesota to be a channel for His love to flow to this Kogi woman of Mamarongo, high in the mountains of northern Colombia.

Roberto and Gloria play with chick.

Dick Carlson
goes to war.
W.W.I., US Navy.

Dick catches while
brother Eddie bats.

Chapter 5

A Murder Planned

South Dakota, North Dakota
1918-1920

In the Kogi language, time and space are closely related. To say that something happened in a spot ten minutes walking time away, or to say that something happened ten minutes ago, one uses the same verb ending. Mamarongo of the Sierra Nevada of Santa Marta seems far removed in time and space from Minneapolis, or even from the bustling town of Cienega, which, located at the foot of the mountains, is the Western gateway to the Sierra Nevada de Santa Marta. However, to really understand how the Stendal family happened to be in Mamarongo, we need to go even further back in time and farther away.

One chilly autumn day, a stocky young man could be seen trudging along a dusty country road near the border of North and South Dakota. His handsome face was twisted into an ugly scowl as his large, well-callused right hand fingered the handle of a revolver that had been hastily thrust into his overcoat pocket. World War I was recently at an end, and some six months before, Dick Carlson had hastily doffed his sailor uniform in Minneapolis and caught a train to the small South Dakota village near the home of his sweetheart, Eva Winburn.

He had first seen Eva some eight years before, when her older brother, Ovie, had brought him to the Winburn home for dinner. Dick would never forget the delicious meal served by Mrs. Winburn, quite a contrast to the meager fare offered at the neighboring farm where he was the hired man. The fried chicken and country gravy served with potatoes and fresh leaf lettuce out of the family garden had reminded him of the delicious food served by his own tiny Swedish immigrant mother back in Minneapolis. Dick had enjoyed grade school and had longed to attend high school, but his huge, carpenter father, looking at the high school boys in their dark suits and stiffly starched white shirts and neckties had gruffly proclaimed that no son of his was going to be a sissy and had immediately gotten 16-year-old Dick a grown man's job in heavy construction. A year later, seeking a change, city- bred Dick had come to South Dakota to work as a farm hand.

Impressed as Dick had been by the good Winburn food, what had really caught his attention was 15-year-old Eva. An accomplished horsewoman, Eva was an outdoors girl who broke and trained her own horses, riding in races and quadrilles in local fairs. Now, as Dick passed a dried-up cornfield, the brown stalks made a rustling sound in the early fall wind. It had been in a cornfield such as this that Dick had first noticed Eva. She had been wearing a middy blouse and a long, divided riding skirt; her cheeks flushed pink from the brisk chilly breeze. With a .22 rifle in one hand, she had proudly shown him the gopher tails from her morning's hunt. (South Dakota paid a bounty on these rodents.) Dick could well remember how he had inwardly resolved, "That's the girl I'm going to marry someday."

The friendship had progressed as Dick became a frequent visitor to the Winburn homestead that summer. After he had returned to Minneapolis to work as a switchman on the railroad, he continued to make trips to South Dakota to visit the

Winburn family making good friends of Eva's older brothers, Ovie, Charlie, and Omer as well.

Dick's father, the big Swedish carpenter, did not need to worry that his son would be a sissy. Dick was soon a frequent customer in the bars of lower Minneapolis. His quick temper and violent nature involved him in many a bar-room brawl where he soon gained fame as a skillful boxer. His muscular chest and arms gave him a powerful punch while his short, sturdy legs gave him agility. His quick-witted strategy made up for his lack of reach and height, and he was able to win against many a taller opponent.

After the outbreak of World War I in Europe, Dick and his younger brother were quick to enlist in the U.S. Navy. Dick hurried out to South Dakota again, his blond, curly hair and Scandinavian good looks set off to perfection by his new navy blue sailor suit. Saying a fond good-by to Eva, he left her with a ring and a watch, tokens of his love and their intention to marry when he returned.

Lois and Eva show patriotism with their Navy blouses.

He returned to South Dakota at the end of the war jubilantly bragging of his vast capacity to hold liquor and exhibiting an ample vocabulary of salty sailor language. Imagine his consternation when he was greeted by a very different Eva. She returned his ring and watch and told him that the last thing she wanted to do was to marry a hard-drinking, swearing ex-sailor.

Dick's heart was broken. For over eight years, he had counted on marrying Eva. He was not used to having his will crossed. First he had tried to make her jealous by giving the ring and watch to her friend, Lois and when that failed and no amount of pleading would change her mind, he had formed a sinister plan. Yesterday he had purchased a revolver and resolved to kill first Eva and then himself. If she wouldn't marry him, he would see to it that she never married anyone. Now he was on his way to the Winburn farm to carry out the evil deed.

While Dick had been on board ship, shuttling U.S. troops to France amid the dangers of torpedo launching German submarines, Eva too had been having unusual experiences. A community of German-Russian immigrants had come to her town looking for a teacher to help their children learn English, and Eva had volunteered. These German-speaking people had been displaced by the war in Europe, first to Russia, and then they had come to North Dakota with their families, seeking a better life in a new land. With them had come their German language and their German-Russian customs.

Resourceful Eva organized the little one room schoolhouse and devised a system of teaching the children, most of whom did not know one word of English. Her favorite was Martha, an eight-year-old with long, blond braids and big serious eyes. Martha became Eva's constant companion, holding tightly to

Eva with her German – Russian school children

her hand as they walked to and from the schoolhouse set on a hill out on the prairie to Martha's house where Eva boarded. Martha was a quick learner and was soon able to communicate somewhat with Eva in English.

The customs in Martha's home seemed very strange to Eva. Every morning after breakfast, the entire family dropped to their knees, and beginning with the father, and ending with the youngest child who could talk, one by one they lifted their voices in prayer to God in their German language.

While this was taking place, Eva sat quietly in her chair. "Teacher, why don't you pray? begged Martha.

"Shh, I can't! I don't know how!" pleaded Eva, as she squirmed uncomfortably in her straight-backed chair.

"You don't have to learn. It just comes out of your heart." was Martha's reply.

Eva's discomfiture increased as later in the year, Halley's comet appeared in the sky. These simple people assumed that it indicated the second coming of Christ, and night after night ran out in front of the house to welcome Him, excitedly calling out His name in their German language. Eva understood the name, Jesus, in German, and she would run to her room and crouch up in a ball in fear. She couldn't understand how anyone would want Jesus to come back again and disrupt the normal course of life.

The Winburn family was not religious, however several years before this, the dearly loved mother, Ella, had almost died of a ruptured gall bladder. As the gravely ill mother had been lifted into the horse drawn buggy to seek medical aid, the devastated young Eva had prayed, "God, if there is a God, please save my mother, and I will serve you all my life. In due time the mother had returned, but as life returned to normal in the Winburn farmhouse, Eva's busy life had left little time to think about someone so remote as God.

But to these German-Russian immigrants God was not remote. He was an important part of their daily lives. They had no pastor, but on Sundays they gathered in their little chapel. As all prayed silently, finally one man would rise and walk to the pulpit, having been impressed by the Spirit of God that he had the day's message.

When an itinerant pastor arrived late that winter to hold revival meetings, Eva resolved to stay at home. The services were entirely in German, unintelligible to her except for the Bible text, which was read in English. She sensed that something about these people was bothering her tremendously. She felt a heavy conviction of sin and felt as though God and the devil were battling over her soul. However, the first night of the special meetings, before she could escape to her room, the German mother came with a big smile on her face, holding Eva's heavy winter coat, making it plain that Eva was expected to go to the service in the sleigh with the rest of the family. Eva meekly donned the coat and went out to the sleigh.

At the chapel, all the people knelt for prayer, but Martha told Eva to stand when the others knelt, as she was not a believer. Towards the end of the two-week period, Eva felt so terrible standing alone that she could bear it no longer. While the others were praying she dropped to her knees and started crying out to God to save her. At last a sense of peace settled over her, and she knew that she had made contact with the living God.

The impact on Eva was so great that she asked to be taken to her home that very night to tell her family about the tremendous change that had taken place in her life. Awakening them from their sleep, she was surprised and disappointed at their lack of enthusiasm. "You just got excited," stated her father. "I've been to lots of meetings like that. You'll get over it."

"Oh, no, Father," replied Eva. "I've really been changed. Something (she didn't know it was Someone) has come into my heart and into my life."

"Time will tell," said her old father as he rolled over to go back to sleep again. Eva at once knew that the witness of her daily life would be of supreme importance. Eight years later, her father found the same peace during his final illness.

At the end of the school year, Eva returned to her home to live a Christian life before her family. She found work as a clerk in a store and as an operator for the local telephone system. Her faith and devotion to God never waivered, the God she had met through the German-Russian people even though she did not understand their language. This then was the Eva that Dick found when he returned from his service in the U.S. Navy.

My beloved Grandma
Winburn who lived with
us until her death at 87
years of age in 1944.

The grandfather I never
knew, but who found the
Lord on his deathbed through
his daughter Eva's testimony.

My Grandma Carlson
who suffered through
several amputations of
one leg due to gangrene.

My Grandpa Carlson who was
a carpenter accompanied by my
Uncle Eddie who was a fireman.

Chapter 6

The Scales Are Turned

Dick's parents had sent him to confirmation classes at a large Swedish Lutheran church, but all that Dick could remember of the teaching was that on judgment day God would put all of an individual's evil deeds on one side of a scale, and all the good deeds on the other. If the good outweighed the bad, it was heaven; the converse — hell. With this one concept of spiritual values, Dick had decided that already his bad deeds far outweighed any good ones that he could do. He was eternally doomed and might just as well have as good a time as possible before his terrible fate fell.

The road rounded a curve and shot straight as an arrow for a mile or more to the town on whose outskirts the Winburns lived. Dick's features softened. While he had been in the navy boot camp in Michigan, Eva's letters had been frequent and friendly, telling about riding horses bareback in a local fair. Then later, the few that had come to him on the ship, told about the horseless carriage she had bought with her own earnings, a bran new 1916 Model T Ford, the first one in the community. What fun Eva and her friend, Lois, had had. Frightened horses reared on all sides as the strange machine chugged along this same gravel road on which he was walking. Eva had learned to change and fix flat tires and do simple mechanical repairs, as it would be years before there would be a service station in the area.

Eva was an unusual girl and well worth fighting for, Dick mused. Then his broad brow again twisted into a sinister scowl. "If I can't have her, no one else will either," he muttered through clenched teeth, and his hand gripped the cold metal handle of the weapon in his pocket.

As the road neared Eva's home, it passed a bridge spanning a small river. All of a sudden a horrible thought entered his mind: "If I carry out my intention, she will go to heaven, and I will go to hell! I still won't be with her!" With characteristic impulsiveness, he hurled the revolver into the river.

When he arrived in town, Dick headed straight to a telephone to call Eva. Since she was operating the switchboard on the country line, it wasn't too difficult to reach her. He pleaded with her to see him just once more. If nothing could be worked out between them, he promised to return to Minneapolis and leave her to live her life in peace. However Eva had been thoroughly warned by the small town grapevine that Dick was carrying a gun and was threatening to take her life, so she was extremely wary. "The only place I will see you is in a church service," she told him.

Since it was Sunday, both of the churches in town were holding services that evening. Eva was a member of the Wesleyan Methodist whose pastor was noted for his 'hellfire and brimstone' messages. Right across the street was a Congregational church where the preaching was reported to be less dramatic. Dick thought he would feel more comfortable in the Congregational church, so he agreed to meet Eva there for the evening service.

Eva was disappointed as she felt that he would hear a more convincing message in her own church, but she agreed to meet him there. As the Congregational pastor rose to his pulpit to begin his message, a sweating horse pulled up at the door, and a disheveled rider dismounted and ran into the church with a message for the pastor. A parishioner was dying out in the country and requested the pastor's immediate presence. The pastor hesitated only to announce that he would like for the entire congregation to pass in a body to the other church without anyone leaving. Dick and Eva rose with the others and filed across the street to Eva's church.

They were just in time to hear the message, which seemed meant just for Dick. He answered the altar call at the close of the message and kneeling briefly at the altar, arose, shook the pastor's hand, and exclaimed, "Why can't people see it!" In later years Dick was to say that up to this point he thought he had to go to hell for his past sins. This was the first time he had understood that there was forgiveness.

After shaking Dick's hand, the pastor slipped away for a private word with Eva. "I don't believe that this is real," he whispered. "This is probably just an act to get you to marry him." Eva agreed with the pastor. After all, without any really serious sins in her past, she had agonized for two weeks before she felt peace with God. How could Dick with all his bad background and sinful lifestyle be converted so easily and quickly? She told Dick that she did not believe his conversion to be genuine and did not want to see him anymore.

But Dick knew that his life had been changed. The next day, Monday, he was working in Ovie's barber shop in a nearby town. (He had learned to cut hair in order to get a job near Eva.) As he waited for customers, he picked up a novel to read to pass the time as usual. All of a sudden he became extremely disturbed with what he was reading. He smashed the novel against the opposite wall muttering, "Trash! Lies!" and was never to read a fiction book again or allow one to be read in his house, except grudgingly when a school assignment required it.

Since Eva would have nothing to do with him, there was no reason for him to stay in South Dakota. One of the pastors recommended a Bible Institute in Iowa, and he decided it was time to further his educational dreams. Dick thoroughly enjoyed his three years in the Bible College although his sharp, critical mind picked out every flaw in the staff and curriculum. He never returned to his former habits of alcohol and fighting, although he retained his tendency to quick temper and impulsive acts. As judged by his reminiscing in later years, he especially enjoyed the classes in English, both grammar and poetry. To his embarrassment, Dick's photograph with his handsome face and thick, curly, blond hair was chosen as the centerpiece for his class graduation picture, surrounded by individual portraits of his classmates.

After leaving the Institute, he tried preaching for a while, but because he was very reluctant to receive offerings, he soon started using his mechanical genius to earn his living. At the same time he preached every night, either on the street or in a rescue mission (which were then very prevalent in all the large cities). Many times he would stand up on a soapbox and preach on a street corner. Then when a crowd gathered, he would lead them all over to a rescue mission. He was tireless in his efforts, and only needed some four hours of sleep at night. He enjoyed the hearty camaraderie of the rescue mission preachers and prison and jail workers. Many had been converted out of backgrounds even more unsavory than Dick's. He liked to recount his own experiences in the world of saloons and street fights and how he had been delivered through the testimony of a girl he had met while she was shooting gophers in South Dakota.

After a number of years, he started to think of marriage and tried to get interested in the Christian girls of his acquaintance. However Eva's face always came into his mind's eye, and he could feel nothing for the other girls. Back in South Dakota, news came to Eva that Dick Carlson was now preaching on the streets in Cincinnati. She got his address and wrote him a letter. Dick's response was characteristic. "If you want to have anything to do with me," he wrote her, "meet me in Aberdeen (thirty miles from her home) on May 18, 1928, and we will get married. Otherwise forget it." She met him, and they got married that very day in the home of a pastor in Aberdeen, South Dakota.

Eva & Dick in 1928 with their car, a Plymouth.

At the time of their marriage, Dick was working as an elevator constructor for Westinghouse, installing elevators in large buildings throughout the United States. He took his bride to Cincinnati, Ohio, where he had rented a small apartment in a large complex. Thirty-one-year-old Eva found the adjustment to city life overwhelming. Used to the wide-open prairies, seldom, if ever, running into an unfamiliar face, she felt imprisoned in the large apartment building, surrounded by strangers to whom she had been cautioned not to speak. Dick went to work early, then to the mission in the evening, returning in the wee hours to sleep about four hours before going to work again. Eva tried to enter into the mission work with him, but since all her life she had retired to bed about eight p.m., she found it too exhausting. (I believe a heart valve had been damaged by scarlet fever in childhood, and she always needed extra rest.) She soon was overcome by heavy depression, which threatened to envelop her. The only hope she could see was the possibility of having a tiny daughter someday to assuage her loneliness.

From the beginning of her pregnancy there were prob-
lems. The doctor prescribed a drug to prevent a miscarriage
that was constantly threatening. By May 1929, six months
along in the pregnancy, Eva felt well enough to accompany
Dick on a weekend train trip to minister in a distant city. On
the train the pains started again, and she was glad she had
brought her medicine along. However, this time the pains
did not stop, so she took the medicine again. This was re-
peated all weekend, and upon returning to Cincinnati, Eva
was rushed into the hospital in serious condition.

Dick, who was completely uninitiated into maternity and
childbirth procedures, was adamant that his wife not be taken
into the delivery room without him. The hospitals back in
those days had strict rules that barred all husbands from the
delivery room. Not realizing that the doctors were dealing
with a life or death situation, he felt rebuffed and rejected as
the hospital staff rushed to handle the emergency, paying no
attention to him. A glimpse through the swinging doors of
Eva on the delivery table unnerved him completely. He had
lost control of this situation, and he soon lost control of himself. His shouts reverberated through the entire hospital as
his powerful fists tried to break down the delivery room doors.
Later, a subdued Dick purchased a small coffin and disconso-
lately witnessed the burial of his tiny daughter who had died
sometime during the weekend train trip.

Eva was inconsolable at the loss of the baby, and especially as the doctor had told her that because of her age and
the unfortunate experience, it would not be advisable for her
to have any more children. Heavy scars had formed on her
heart as a result of Dick's scandalous behavior in the hospital
at a time when she was in such pain and danger. But in spite
of the doctor's advice, three months later Eva was back in his
office again.

The doctor, who had been appalled by Dick's behavior in
the hospital, felt very sorry for Eva as he confirmed her suspi-
cion that another baby was on its way. "Your only hope," he

told her, "to get through this pregnancy safely and bear a live baby is to go home to your mother, if you have one, and stay with her until this baby is born."

Over Dick's objections, Eva was soon on her way to South Dakota. Since the installation of the elevators in Cincinnati was completed, Westinghouse sent Dick out to Seattle, Washington, to start a new project. The separation was hard on both of them. The tranquility of the farmhouse in South Dakota was frequently interrupted by angry letters from Seattle. Dick's violent rages never lasted long; the raging lion would soon become a softhearted kitten. After posting a letter in a rage at Eva's absence, Dick would soon relent and send flowers by telegraph. In his mind the flowers canceled out the letter, but since the flowers usually arrived first, then days later the letter, the desired effect was not accomplished, and Eva spent her pregnancy in a state of nerves and roller coaster emotions.

Nevertheless, their patience was rewarded as on May 16, 1930, two years after their marriage and exactly a year after the tragic experience in Cincinnati, I was born in Aberdeen, South Dakota. Eva named me Patricia Anne. Dick stayed in Seattle and did not meet his new daughter until Eva took me to Seattle when I was four months old.

Eva and Patty at
6 months old.

Thea Marie Larsen, born in 1870, in Northern Norway. When she married Jonas, the fact that she was a Sami (laplander) was kept under wraps, later Lena spilled the beans to Pat.

Jonas Andersen, born in 1871, came from a prominent family in Mo I Rana.

Chapter 7

Three Answered Prayers

Norway
  1890's

Going back yet further in time and space to the fro-
zen, mountainous land of northern Norway. Sometime during the last decade of the nineteenth century, another young
woman from a different family wrestled with a problem very
similar to the one that Eva Winburn had faced.

In a wooden frame house built high on the grassy slopes
overlooking a deep, icy fjord, Thea Larsen tossed sleeplessly
on her cot. How could she ever explain to her beloved Jonas
that she couldn't marry him? Before Jonas had gone away
to sea, they had made plans to marry after his return. Yesterday his ship had docked. Jonas' thoughtful relative Lena,
had invited Thea to come from her home farther up the rugged, mountainous coast to be her houseguest, to be on hand
to welcome Jonas home again. Last night amid the festivi-
ties of the warm homecoming extended by Jonas' relatives,
there had been no time for them to talk privately, but she
must not delay longer. Today she must break their engagement.

ing the first months after Jonas had boarded the sailing vessel, Thea had occupied herself outside of working hours
with preparations for her coming wedding, knitting and em-
broidering lovely items for the new home that she and Jonas
planned to form. But then something had happened that
changed her life forever. Some strange travelers had come
to the sleepy little fishing village where Thea lived. These
visitors were earnest young men whose hearts were burning
with a message from God. It was not enough, said they, to
be baptized and confirmed in the State church. One must
have a living and personal relationship with Jesus Christ.

Many in the little village had responded to their invitation
to confess and turn from their sins and dedicate their lives to
God. Among them was Thea, a sturdy, attractive girl in her
mid-twenties. Soon her spare hours were spent in the small
Lutheran Free Church whose membership was growing
weekly. On Sundays with her hair pulled back tightly and
braided neatly into one braid which hung down the middle of
her back, her intense gray eyes sparkling in her strong, dia-
mond shaped face, her Bible tucked under one arm, she
trudged up the mountainside through rain or snow to join
with those who worshipped God in spirit and truth as she
did. Soon her life centered on her newfound faith and the
activities in the little church. Now she felt that she could not
join herself in marriage to a man — no matter how dearly
beloved — who did not know Jesus Christ in the way that she
now did. Especially not a man such as Jonas, who was noted
for his heavy drinking, having fame for being able to walk a
straight line with a keg of liquor on his shoulder even after a
night of indulgence.

Thea rose from her bed, rubbing her burning, sleepless
eyes. The first gray hint of dawn could be seen from the
window outlining the shapes of the steep mountains border-
ing the fjord. As she turned from the window, a faint knock
at the bedroom door startled her. "Thea, Thea," a whispered voice called. "Are you awake? Please get up! I must
speak with you privately before the others arise."

Quickly Thea finished dressing and cautiously opened the door. It was Jonas, his handsome, weather-beaten face drawn into a worried frown. Taking her arm, he pulled her over to a small wooden settee in an alcove near the guest room. "My dear Thea, he started in a low voice with a serious look on his face, "Believe me, I don't want to hurt you, but I must tell you that there has been a tremendous change in my life since I saw you last. I am no longer the same Jonas that you knew before. When I left you here, I was completely worldly-minded, as you well know. I thought of nothing more than the here and now, the daily pleasures of this life. However now all this is changed.

"On board our ship there was a young man who was so different. To him God was not remote, a Being who stayed aloof from us humans and was only contacted occasionally through the clergy in the church. Oh, no! To him God was real and living and involved in his daily life. At first I thought this young man to be strange and ridiculous. I joined with our shipmates in tormenting him with jokes and insults. But seeing the good nature with which he bore our jibes, I began to respect him.

"A few weeks later, a tremendous storm broke over our ship. We were all frightened and despaired of our lives, yet this young sailor faced impending death with calmness and faith. I realized that all he said was true. In the days following the storm, he began to call us together for Bible study and prayer. One by one my shipmates and I found the same personal faith in God that we had seen in our companion.

"And now, Thea dear, I must tell you that my life does not belong to me anymore. I have given it to God. Much as I hate to do so, I feel that I must break our engagement."

"Oh, Jonas!" cried Thea. "I have given my life to Him too. I have lain awake all night searching for words to tell you that I could not marry a man who did not know my Lord as I now know Him."

"Can it be possible!" exclaimed Jonas, "That He has answered my prayers for you already!"

"Or maybe," suggested Thea, "He has answered my prayers for you."

A short time later, when Lena came around to serve her guests tiny cups of delicious coffee, sweet and strong, as is the Scandinavian custom, she found a very happy Thea and Jonas planning their marriage and the Christian home they would establish. Jonas found employment in the mines, and they both took a very active part in the little Lutheran Free Church that Thea had helped found in her town, *Mo i Rana*.

Thea was soon very busy raising four daughters and one son. Warm woolen stockings and colorful sweaters and mittens were all knit by hand. Nutritious meals of fish fresh from the icy waters of the fjord and potatoes from the fields up in the mountains were prepared. For special treats, they had beef or fruits. The home was extremely strict and church centered. Worldly diversions were not allowed. The children stood in respectful awe of their serious, hardworking father, and their resourceful, indomitable mother.

Jenny's Baby Picture.

Jenny, and her sisters,
Petra, Lotte, Molla.

When the oldest girl, Jenny, finished eighth grade, and had been confirmed in the little church, Thea drew her aside for a serious talk. The mother lovingly but firmly explained that Jenny must now earn her own living. The family was poor and could not continue to support a child who had finished all the secular and religious education that the small hamlet could offer. A position had been secured for Jenny, caring for the young children of a well-to-do family. Jenny was horrified. It had never occurred to her that at fourteen years of age she would have to leave home and earn her own living. As the oldest of five children, she was experienced in childcare, but to her that was a most unappealing occupation. That summer Jenny was taken by her employers to a resort area in southern Norway to watch the children while the parents vacationed.

One night Jenny was awakened from her sleep by music. Stealing softly from the nursery, she found herself on a balcony overlooking a brightly lighted area where elegantly dressed men and women were moving in a stately dance to beautiful music. Jenny was hypnotized by the beauty of the spectacle. Night after night, she crouched in the shadows on the balcony, transfixed by the colors, lights, and the gracefulness of the dancers. In the long summer afternoons, the vacationers passed their time with various card games, several of which Jenny and her charges learned to play.

Finally the summer came to an end, and with mixed feelings Jenny returned to her home in northern Norway. Upon her return, Jenny tried to share with Thea the beautiful experience she had enjoyed watching the dancers, but Thea was horrified. "Oh, my dear child!" she cried in alarm. "You must not watch things like that! It is sinful! It is of the devil!"

Jenny felt horrible. How could something so beautiful be so wicked?" she wondered. To pass the dreary hours of the long, northern winter evenings, she painstakingly fashioned a set of playing cards by hand, drawing in the tiny details as best she could remember. At last the deck was complete, and calling her sisters together, she started teaching them the games she had learned at the vacation resort. But when Thea discovered her young daughters playing cards, her rage knew no bounds. Jenny was severely punished, and the cards were thrown in the fire.

A fiery rebellion was kindled in Jenny's heart. Surely her infallible, indomitable mother was wrong for once. She soon moved to the city of Tronheim where she joined other girls from her area who worked in the sewing factories. As she distanced herself from her family, she also distanced herself from the strict upbringing her parents had given her. After a few years an opportunity arose for her to emigrate to America, and Jenny left Norway, putting even more distance between herself and her parent's strict religion.

Arriving in Minneapolis where a former neighbor family from *Mo i Rana* had agreed to give her board and room, Jenny changed her name to Jean and avoided religion as much as possible. She found work sewing in a factory and frequented social activities that were organized by the immigrants from Norway. She soon met a young man of Norwegian ancestry, and after several months of courtship, they were married in 1925.

Jenny at
14 years.

Jean T. Stendal, worked
many years for Honeywell
in Minneapolis.

Russell T. Stendal,
worked as a train engineer.

Russell Stendal, a handsome, mild-mannered, sociable youth, was a splendid dancer and fair violinist. Together they enjoyed the social life of the Norwegian clubs in Minneapolis and St. Paul. Jean was thrifty and industrious and managed their lives well. Frequent letters from Thea in Norway urged her to remember her early training and seek the Lord but went unheeded until tragedy struck.

In due time Jean became pregnant, but being advised that prenatal maternity visits were a waste of money, frugal Jean did not "waste" the money and arrived at a Minneapolis hospital in labor and suffering from serious toxemia. As her labor progressed, it was discovered that her pelvis was too narrow to accommodate the birth of the infant. Terrified Russell, pacing the hospital corridor, was asked to choose between the life of his wife and that of his baby. He chose Jean, and the baby was allowed to die and was removed piecemeal. This was standard procedure before the days of safe C- Sections.

After this dreadful experience, Jean planned to follow the doctor's advice to avoid further pregnancies. However sociable, friendly Russell was always looking into baby carriages and raving over their friends' children in a way that tore at Jean's heart. In her anguish, Jean remembered the story of Hannah and Samuel in the Bible. Jean went to God in prayer, asking for a son and promising to give him back to God as Hannah had done with Samuel.

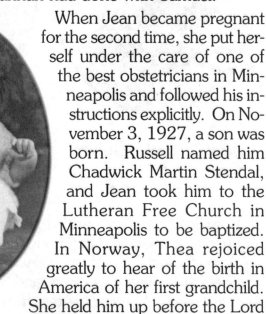

Baby Chad.

When Jean became pregnant for the second time, she put herself under the care of one of the best obstetricians in Minneapolis and followed his instructions explicitly. On November 3, 1927, a son was born. Russell named him Chadwick Martin Stendal, and Jean took him to the Lutheran Free Church in Minneapolis to be baptized. In Norway, Thea rejoiced greatly to hear of the birth in America of her first grandchild. She held him up before the Lord daily in prayer for over forty years.

Toddler Chad with goat cart.

Young Chad in Navy suit.

Chad in his boy scout uniform.

Chad with his cousin Rosemary.

Thea lived
in Mo I
Rana,
Norway.

Jonas and Thea with Jenny's sister Molla.

John was born in 1870 as Johan Johansen in Norway. When he came to the USA, he changed his last name to Stendal, the place where he had lived in Norway. His half-brother was Carl Martin "C.M." Stendal who owned the Stendal Shoe Store in downtown Minneapolis for many years.

John & Magda Stendal.

Magdalina Asbjornsen, born in 1877, was a German-Jew, who had to flee Germany due to persecution. She arrived in Norway at the house of friends who were moving to the USA, she decided to come with them. John & Magda had 4 children. Here she is with Russell, Chad's father, married Jenny.

Young Santiago circa 1948

Chapter 8

A Life Is Saved

Palomino of the Sierra, Colombia
1928 (approximately)

Now about the same time as the birth of Chad, but
in space far away, all the way down south to the Kogi village
of Palomino, located in northern Colombia in the middle of
the Sierra Nevada of Santa Marta. This village is the tradi-
tional center of the Kogi tribe, three days by rugged foot trail
from the Kogi village of Mamarongo. Here we will witness
another beginning that has a direct bearing on the presence
of the Stendal family in Mamarongo in the year 1968.

The first pale light of dawn was breaking over the rugged
mountain peaks, illuminating the white wisps of cotton-like
fog hanging in the hollows of the valley, and the grayer, more
transparent vapor that emanated from the two round, mush-
room-like huts clinging to the steep western slope of the
mountain. Inside one of the huts, a small, brown woman
squatted by the open cooking fire, oblivious to the smoke
that filled the upper part of the hut and seeped out through
the palm-thatched roof. A clay pot filled to the brim with
chunks of white manioc and small, green bananas was bub-
bling merrily over the brightly blazing fire sending spurts of

water sizzling into the flames. But nothing except the cooking pot was merry in *Maldia's* hut this morning.

The woman's large, brown eyes glanced around the interior of the circular mud house. Over to her left in the shadows, her grandson, three-month-old Santiago, wailed with hunger. His mother, *Shenieka* lay on her side on a piece of flattened tree bark, her knees drawn up to her chest in fetal position. Her head was covered with a thin, soiled blanket. It would not be long before her spirit would leave her body and take wing to the high mountain country, there to join with the other recently departed spirits making the cold, moist snow that covered the bare, rocky peaks like thatch covered the peaked roofs of the Kogi houses.

Small *Sama* sat silently on the dirt floor near her mother's head. Grief and fear showed in her round, brown eyes, but she made no sound. Her small arms ached from holding the screaming baby, Santiago, but now, since she could not quiet his hungry cries, she had laid him in his wrappings by the wall of the house and turned to look at her dying mother. She could do nothing but sit in miserable, silent vigil.

Maldia knew that with the death of her daughter, *Shenieka*, *Huilde* her present husband and son-in-law, who was even now chanting in the nearby men's house in a last desperate attempt to convince the spirits to spare *Shenieka's* life, would wander off to find another family with a marriageable daughter to cook his food, pick his coca leaves, and bear his children. *Maldia* did not know her own age, but she was beginning to feel the burden of years upon her frail body. It was most unlikely that she would bear another child. *Huilde* had come to live with her some years ago after the death of old Vicente, *Sheneika's* father. He had come to be her husband, but also to wait for her daughter, *Sheneika*, to reach puberty. It had been an unexpected surprise that *Maldia* had given birth to little one-year-old Jose.

Turning, she looked at her child. Tightly wrapped in a torn piece of an ancient hammock, he had been placed in his *busu,* the bag in which Kogi mothers carry their babies suspended from their heads as they go about their chores. The *busu* was now hung from a wooden peg protruding from a pole of the house frame. He too was silent, burning with fever and too weak to cry. *Maldia* had done all she could. She had set his naked, burning body on her bare feet in the doorway of the house and doused him with cold river water, letting the chilly evening breeze cool his rash-covered body, but it had not helped. His breathing had become very shallow and labored. It was the dreaded *hubi hubi,* (labored, shallow breathing that almost always leads to death in a child). Now he was exhausted. He too would be buried today in his *busu,* and she would be deserted and childless.

Maldia had buried many babies in her lifetime. She had long ago fulfilled the quota of ten babies that every Kogi woman is expected to bear. But always before there had been the hope of more to come, and always there had been *Sheneika. Sheneika,* one of the babies born to *Maldia* long ago, had been a good seed. She had not succumbed to the illnesses and epidemics that had taken the others, but this last sickness with the fever and red rash had overcome her, weakened as she was by recent childbirth. Now in the same day *Maldia* would bury her two remaining children. *Sama, Sheneika's* first-born, belonged to *Huilde.* (Kogi children are designated at birth to belong to one of the parents, not to both.) She was his pride and joy, his only daughter. He could hardly wait until she was old enough to marry, and he would have a son-in-law to serve him. *Maldia* could expect nothing in the future from *Sama.*

The wailing of little Santiago, her grandchild grew more frantic. He too must die soon as his mother's breasts had been dry for days. The baby's incessant wailing increased *Maldia's* own discomfort. Her engorged breasts reacted physically to the baby's cry. Her own child had not emptied them well since the measles had struck him. Suddenly an idea occurred to her. Why should she not save little Santiago? Was he too not her own flesh and blood? He belonged to

Shenieka. Huilde already had a son by a previous wife. Santiago was a hardy child, a good seed.

She lifted him from where he lay beside his dying mother. She loosened his soiled wrappings, pieces of torn cloth from discarded adult clothing. The skin was peeling from his tiny knees and elbows as he had fruitlessly thrashed in his struggle for life, rubbing them against the harsh cloth. He was soaking wet with urine and covered with feces. A small, black dog, whose skinny body revealed every rib, eagerly inserted his head into the loosened wrappings and quickly devoured the fecal material, his pink tongue expertly cleaning the tiny buttocks. Removing the soiled cloth, old *Maldia* scraped it with a stiff, green plantain skin to remove any remaining solid waste, and then threw it over the side of the mud wall to dry. Taking down a dry cloth and wrapping the tiny form tightly, she placed him to her breast where he sucked noisily, his whimpers subsiding into sighs of satisfaction. Santiago Dingula's life had been saved.

Old woman with her baby and cat. Maldía was approx the same age as this woman, when Santiago was a baby.

Chapter 9

Santiago's Childhood

Years passed, and the days fell into a routine for young Santiago. Every morning after an early breakfast of boiled green plantains and taro root he trudged to the fields behind Sama, his sister, and Maldia, his *haba wezhu* (old mother, grandmother). Huilde had returned to the farm after fulfilling his bride service for a new wife, who now lived in a small round hut near the men's house over by the sugar cane field, while Maldia had her abode farther up the steep slope near the coca bushes.

While Huilde chopped down the large trees during the dry months of January and February and saw to the burning of the fields just before the rains started again in March, most of the day to day farming was left to the women and children. In mid-March holes were made in the earth with a large pole, and several kernels of corn were planted in each one. Young shoots which grow around the bases of the plantain and banana trees were set out so as to mature at intervals of time, providing an unending supply of both the cooking plantains and eating bananas. The white, starchy root vegetables of manioc (the nonpoisonous variety) and taro with its large elephant ear leaf were carefully tended. At least twice during the year all fields must be cleared of weeds and undergrowth by cutting away undesirable vegetation with a sharp machete.

Much of this work fell to young Santiago and Santo, an older son of Huilde who lived with him in the men's house.

Old *Maldia* had surprised everyone by bearing one more child, a son named *Samanu*. While she still went to the fields every morning, the baby hanging from her head in the *busu*, the old woman depended more and more on Santiago and Sama for the routine farming tasks.

The first drops of rain that fell each day around noon signaled the time to leave the fields. Backs bent beneath the loads of farm produce — green plantain, taro, manioc — their small feet padded rapidly over the steep footpath with bare toes gripping into the soft mud for traction on the moist perpendicular slopes. In addition to the loaded *gamas* supported from their foreheads, Maldia's strong neck muscles also supported the baby in his *busu.* He had now grown miserable by the many hours in the fields, hungry, urine soaked, and overheated. Sometimes Maldia worked with the baby on her back, thus cutting off the circulation of blood in the little legs squeezed between the *busu* and the mother's body. Kogi babies are not very fussy. They soon learn that crying brings no relief from their discomfort. Sometimes the sleeping child was laid on the grass where he was at the mercy of insects, biting gnats and crawling ants.

As she scurried along the uneven muddy trail, Maldia's hands were busily occupied making carrying bags, the Kogi *gama*. The Kogis do not use baskets or other containers but use the *gama* whenever receptacles are needed. While most are made of jute fiber, each man also wears one made of cotton thread, the *sugamei*.

Most days they arrived at the shelter of their *hui* (house) before the daily downpour began. Maldia would remove the baby from the *busu*, loosen his urine soaked wrappings, and let the naked little brown body squirm and roll on the earthen floor while she cleaned the rags and hung them to dry on the rafters or over the wall of the house. Then with a small, worn machete she started slitting the skins of the green plantains, heedless of the sticky white liquid, which clung to her fingers and palms, staining the skin a perpetual black. Mean-while Santiago built up the smoldering fire, while Sama threw any uneaten food to the chickens and rinsed out the cooking pot. Soon the kettle was busily boiling over the fire, covered with a green leaf from a banana tree.

A six-years-old is expected to cook lunch for the whole family

Usually the noon meal consisted of boiled green plantains with taro root or manioc and *panela* (crude brown sugar) water, but occasionally a small bird, a snail, or a mouse added protein to their soup. Many Kogis raised pigs or chickens or even occasionally butchered a cow or ox to provide protein, but Maldia and Huilde were content with their starchy diet. Their bodies long ago had adapted to function with a minimum of protein. Sama and Santiago's small bodies were now learning to do the same. Their bone structure was not growing to full potential but was retarded in development, lacking vitamins and calcium as well as protein. Sama's permanent teeth were erupting, but her jawbone and face were too small to receive them, causing the teeth to jam together giving her face a grotesque, old-woman look. The children's leg and arm bones were very short making them look years younger than their ages, but their muscles were strong and resilient from wielding the machete and running up and down the mountain sides loaded with heavy burdens.

Huilde did not come to the door of Maldia's hut for food very often anymore. The aging woman could not be ex-

pected to bear more children. His attentions must now go to
the new young wife whose fertility was at its peak. While old
Maldia enjoyed Santiago's presence in her hut, she knew
that he must learn to be a man by closer association with his
father. He must soon go to sleep in the men's house to begin
to absorb the ways of the Kogi male.

After the rain, Maldia, Sama and Santiago left the hut
once more, the women to the stream, their *gamas* filled with
gourds to bring water, and he to the woods with his machete
to bring firewood. After the evening meal, much the same as
at noon, old Maldia spun jute thread, rolling the fiber against
her bare thigh with her right hand and winding it up on a
spindle, a stick with one end resting on the ground, twirled
by her left hand. Sama worked on a jute carrying bag using
a large needle and a stitch just like a buttonhole stitch. Her
sensitive fingers found the loops in the semi-darkness by a
sense of touch.

Santiago stared into the dying fire and thought about the
future. Someday he would be a man. The thought filled him
with fear and also a certain anticipation. There must be more
to the world than this valley. He would like to see what lay
on the other side of the ridges, which so effectively blocked
his view. With manhood would come freedom to leave Huilde
and Maldia and travel to distant Kogi villages. He had heard
of Don Diego over the mountains to the north, also San Fran-
cisco and San Miguel, the two largest Kogi villages with over
100 families in each. With manhood would also come the
knowledge of the Kogi religious heritage.

As he gazed into the fire each evening, Santiago dreamed
of the world beyond his valley. Some from his village had
crossed the *gexa*, the high mountain country above the tree
line. Braving death by sudden snowstorm or wild beasts,
they had passed through the domain of the recent dead, the
snow, and descended to the fertile lands on the western side
of the rocky peaks, founding the new Kogi settlements, San
Andres, Cherua, and another western Mamarongo.

Two boys about his own age from Mamarongo were even now in training to be *mamas* (the priest shaman of the Kogis). They were kept in the secret ceremonial house of Mama Pedro farther up the valley. Santiago had seen them once when he had carried a message to Mama Pedro from old Maldia. The acolytes must stay inside the hut in the daytime as no sunlight may touch their bodies. They slept during the daytime hours and spent the nights sitting at the feet of Mama Pedro learning the stories, dances, and chants, which were the heritage of the Kogis.

It was said that one of the boys, Ignacio, was an apt pupil. Perhaps he would learn the entire wealth of Kogi knowledge and be able to control the world of nature, bringing the sun up in the morning, bringing the dry season at the end of December so that the fields could be burned and planted, making the seeds sprout in March and April. To the Kogis had been entrusted the responsibility of maintaining the world of nature. The fear of each Kogi was that the mamas would die before their store of knowledge had been passed on to a successor. (Since they did not have a written language, this was the only way to preserve their lore.) It was generally agreed that the younger generation was not what the older one had been. The youth were negligent and stupid, not absorbing all that their elders had known. With each generation there was irreparable loss of Kogi knowledge. It was a great tragedy due to the dullness and inattention of the young.

Why had he not been sent to learn? wondered the young Santiago. He would have diligently learned each word that was taught. He would not have let one bit of the *muligabba* (Kogi wisdom) be lost. The boy's forehead puckered into a worried frown as he considered such serious matters. He knew why he had not been sent to be trained as a mama. Besides the fact the Huilde had little interest in spiritual aspirations, Old Maldia needed him. She had saved his life as a baby, and she had no other child to help her. Sama belonged to Huilde and was only allowed to live with Maldia

until puberty when she would attract a son-in-law for Huilde.
Then Sama must live with Huilde's new wife close to the
men's house. No, Santiago could not be spared for intellec-
tual pursuits.

A shower of sparks suddenly shot upward from a large
log, breaking into Santiago's reverie. Oh, well, he shrugged.
It was best this way. He would not have liked to be cooped
up in a dark hut all day. He would have missed old Maldia
and the other children. The candidates for shaman were not
allowed to see women, not even their own mother, for years
at a time. Their diet also was most restricted. They must eat
neither salt nor products of the cow. But the *muldigabba*,
how he would love to study the *muldigabba*, to know all the
wisdom and knowledge of his people.

Mama Nacio with his wife and child. He was in training when
Santiago was a child. It was he who gave permission
for the Stendal family to live in Mamarongo,
following his miraculous healing

Chapter 10

Huilde's Men's House

On other evenings as Santiago sat beside the fire, he thought of the different peoples who lived beyond the ridges: The Kogi were the real ones, but there were also the others. The Arhuacos, those strong, tall ones who indecently exposed their bulging arm muscles, whose arrogance deeply offended the Kogis; the Malayos so much like themselves, but whose language they could not understand, whose women tied red cloths on their heads and sometimes wore two dresses, one on top of the other so that both of their shoulders would be covered; and then there were the *non-Kogis*, those noisy outsiders who were not real people at all, but younger brothers, created later after the Indians, the real ones.

Santiago had actually seen several *non-Kogis* once, tall strangers with short, colorful shirts stuffed into dark colored pants, their feet covered by black, rubber boots, their hair cut short. Strangest of all, one had bushy hair growing under his nose. They had seemed to be lost, but Huilde had crossly sent them away, quickly indicating the trail, which led down out of the mountains.

These boisterous intruders had no respect for the spirit owners of the natural world. They chopped down trees, picked up rocks, and cut grass as they pleased with no thought of placating the rightful owners. Worse yet, they actually disturbed the burial places of the ancients, taking pottery and carved stone pieces to the lowlands to sell. These *non-Kogis* were sure to incur the wrath and retaliation of the spirits against them all. They must be kept out of the Kogi area by any means.

""My son!" Old Maldia's voice broke into his thoughts. "Tomorrow you will move to the men's house to sleep with your father. You must learn the ways of the (Kogi men)."

With mixed feelings Santiago stretched out on his mat of bark. Vainly he tried to pull his legs up under his threadbare tunic for warmth, but it was too short to do much good. Wrapping his hands, which he had slipped inside his tunic around his upper arms, he turned towards the fire and closed his eyes. Tomorrow he would sleep in the men's house.

The next day, his one extra garment was quickly stuffed into a carrying bag, and Santiago was on his way. He had no other possession except the short machete that he carried in his hand. He had gathered several days' firewood for Maldia before he started down the narrow trail. Crossing the crystal clear stream at the foot of the hill, he climbed up the muddy bank on the other side, the soft clay oozed between his bare toes, which dug in to give him a foothold on the slippery surface. Breaking out on a small rise, the trail sloped sharply downward and to the left, following the configuration of the terrain through cultivated land, then through a wooded area. A sharp turn to the right across another small stream brought Santiago to a long, grassy slope, Huilde's pasture. Climbing the hill and crossing a level area to the other side of the pasture, he would find the men's house.

Santiago hesitated a moment. Behind him was the familiar routine of life that he had always known. Maldia and Sama would have the cooking pot on the fire by now for an early supper. Baby Samanu would be sitting on the ground or toddling around the familiar round hut. Soon supper would be ready in Maldia's cozy hut. A sigh escaped him. He looked up the grassy green hill. A large mango tree cast a long shadow across the trail, and a lazy, white *buey* (ox) chewed its cud contentedly. Ahead was the new world of the men's house: his father, his half-brother, Santos, the lifestyle of the Kogi male, but most of all the *muldigabba,* the *muldigabba* of the ancient mother. This is what he wanted to learn. His father would teach him. Resolutely, the young boy turned his back on the familiar past and started up the grassy incline. Six years of mountain walking had strengthened his calf muscles into firm masses. His young body bent forward to accommodate the weight of the *gama* full of *manioc*, hanging from a head strap, which passed over his thick, matted, curly black hair. Maldia had sent this to Huilde from the field at her end of the farm. Quickly reaching the summit of the hill, he crossed the level pasture where a brown cow stared at him with wary eyes, and before him was Huilde's men's house.

The round structure was built of poles with old pieces of squeezed sugar cane enclosing the walls two thirds of the way up. In the center of the house stood the *trapiche*, the sugar cane mill, as the house also served to grind sugar cane on occasion. The doorway was larger and wider than in most Kogi houses, as it must accommodate the *buey* (ox) to turn the *trapiche*. By now the sun had sunk behind the mountain, and while a faint glow of twilight remained outside, the interior of the house was dark.

Entering through the doorway, Santiago's eyes strained to make out a hammock on the other side of the *trapiche*.

"Father," greeted the boy, according to Kogi courtesy.

A grunt came from the hammock, acknowledging the greeting. Passing to the side of the hammock, the boy let the carrying bag full of *manioc* fall to the ground. He could hardly lift the heavy load with his arms. Kogi children have far more strength in their neck and back muscles than in their arms, but as best he could, he offered the *manioc* to his father. Another grunt from the hammock acknowledged the gift, and a hand holding a stick indicated toward the door opposite the side of the house where the boy had entered. Santiago moved the *manioc* to the door.

There seemed nothing more to do, so the boy squatted on the damp ground. A small fire was burning near the hammock and cast a dim light over this half of the house. The figure in the hammock was motionless except for a scraping of the stick against the rim of a pear-shaped gourd he held in the other hand. From time to time he placed the stick in his mouth, then into the interior of the gourd, then to his mouth again.

A figure entered the doorway where the bag of *manioc* still sat. It was Santos with a long piece of firewood on his shoulder.

"Older brother," Santiago greeted him, jumping to his feet.

With an affirmative nasal grunt the older boy recognized the greeting.

The firewood was thrown along the wall of the house, and Santos joined Santiago squatting beside the fire. Darkness had fallen now. There was no moon. The boys sat in silence. All was inky blackness except for the small glow from the fire.

Suddenly Huilde arose from the hammock. He spat a huge wad of green leaves from his mouth as he headed for the door. "Let's eat", he mumbled to the boys as he passed through the doorway into the night.

Santiago followed his father and half-brother down the far side of the hill for some twenty paces until another dwelling rose up out of the darkness. It had the usual round mud walls and peaked thatched roof. The entrance was towards the men's house and was low and narrow. Huilde stopped outside the doorway and sat on a low, flat rock that lay just to one side of the entrance. Santos sat on a broad log of firewood that had been placed on the other side of the doorway. Santiago hesitated a moment, then squatted on the ground beside his father.

A woman came to the door. She was small and slender. In her hands was an earthen pot covered with a large, green leaf from a banana tree. She set the pot before Huilde and retired into the interior of the house. Huilde lifted the leaf from the pot and a white vapor arose. With his fingers Huilde removed a chunk of white vegetable and handed it across the doorway to Santos, then one to Santiago. It was taro, a root vegetable similar to potatoes, but with a slight toxic quality. The three munched noisily, washing down the dry starch with sips of the liquid in which it had been cooked, and slurped from a rounded section of gourd, which they passed from hand to hand. A small, green, boiled plantain was also handed to Santiago, then the pot was passed inside to the woman.

She was *Malgalita,* the woman Huilde had married after Seneika's death. According to Maldia, Malgalita could do nothing properly. Santiago felt repugnance towards his mother's replacement. He knew her by sight of course, but sensing Maldia's dislike, Malgalita seldom visited the other end of the farm. Inside the house, a baby wailed. After awhile a half-gourd of *panela* water was passed out. Huilde drank first, then Santos. By the time the gourd was passed to Santiago little was left, but he eagerly downed the few remaining drops. The gourd was handed inside, and Huilde rose to leave. The boys slipped into the dark woods to take care of their necessities, then followed Huilde into the men's house. He was already in the hammock with a wad of coca leaves in his mouth and had resumed the rhythmic scraping of the stick on the gourd.

Santos pulled a bark mat down from the rafters and laid it by the fire. Carefully he placed the ends of two long logs into the fire. As the night wore on, Santos would gradually push these logs toward the center. He partially blocked the two doorways of the house with pieces of wood, and then lay down on the mat on the side nearest the fire. Santiago timidly lay on the other edge of the mat, as far away from his brother as possible. The flames died down to glowing, red coals.

Santiago lay still, but his eyes would not close. The wind whistled through the open part of the doorway around the silent figures and the trapiche and out the other side. Cold drafts of air entered under the roof where the wall was open. This shelter was not friendly and cozy like Maldia's hut. There had been no fascinating talk of the *muldigabba* around the fire that evening.

A *nabbi* (jaguar) could easily come through that doorway in the night, thought Santiago. A gnawing feeling, not entirely due to hunger, grew in his stomach. Was this the life of the *asigi*, the Kogi male? He longed to snuggle up to Santos for warmth, but reserve held him back. Santos was almost a man. He already wore the tunic of a Kogi man with long sleeves that came below the elbow. All he lacked was the pants to complete the Kogi adult costume. The boy bravely huddled himself together and tried to generate warmth from his small body. He consoled himself with the thought that on the weekend they would be going to the big reunion at the central village site. There he would hear the *muldigabba* from the *mamas.* At last, with eyes half open, he drifted into a troubled sleep.

Chapter 11

Santiago Grows Up

The unthinkable had happened. Sama was dead. Almost a year had passed since Santiago had gone to live with his father. This morning at daybreak old Maldia had arrived with small Samanu on her back bringing the terrible news.

The child had been ailing for sometime, although no one had noticed the first signs of parasite infection and anemia. Never very healthy since the death of her mother, Sama had grown paler and thinner each day. Santiago had been astounded one day several months before. He had been sent to Maldia's hut with a large bag of *panela*. Sama had been alone in the house, lying on her mat too sick to accompany Maldia to the fields. Her hair had become thin and scanty with a reddish tinge; her face was puffy and yellow; her limbs had become grotesquely thin, and her abdomen was large and bloated. The years of malnutrition, especially protein deficiency, had taken their toll. Now a heavy hookworm infection in addition to the normal parasites such as ameba and roundworm were bringing Sama's short life to a speedy end. Maldia had visited the *mama* with gifts of eggs and chickens, and Huilde had even taken a pig, but the dances and colored stones of the *mama* had not availed. Sama had died.

Huilde's grief expressed itself in rage toward old Maldia. Why had she allowed Sama to die? In just a few more years she would have been old enough to attract a mate. Then Huilde would have had a son-in-law to serve him and care for him in his old age and replace Santos, who in a few years must leave Huilde to serve a father-in-law. Why had he entrusted the child to Maldia? He should have brought her to Malgalita in spite of the fact that Maldia was the child's maternal grandmother. In his anguish over the loss of his "social security," Huilde continued railing on Maldia. It must be her fault. Had she been planting without the permission of the spirit world? Did he have to do everything? Yes, as far as securing permissions from the spirit world, it was up to him. Women played no part in this aspect of Kogi life.

Huilde always felt under a heavy burden of indebtedness to the spirit owners of the land. He spent as much time as possible in his hammock, ruminating his coca (rolling a wad of leaves around with his tongue) and meditating, seeking to feel unity with the spirit world. On reunion nights he went to the village, leaving Santiago at home to help Malgalita and to make sure that other men did not visit her in his absence. He fasted and went without sleep to help pay his debt to the spirits for using the land. But his asceticism was never enough. Now they had taken his daughter, his only hope for the future.

True, Malgalita's new baby was a girl, but she would probably die too as had all of Malgalita's previous offspring. He went sullenly down the trail towards Maldia's house to bury poor Sama's wasted body.

Kogi woman tests the liquid panela.

Santiago sadly watched them go down the trail. Santos followed his father with a *cabador*, a simple tool to dig a hole for the burial. He must stay and help Malgalita make *panela* (brown sugar blocks). The sugar cane had been cut the previous afternoon, and the juice must be extracted this morning. Now Malgalita was hitching the big, white ox to the *trapiche* in the middle of the men's house. Ordinarily Malgalita would not have been allowed to enter the men's house, but since this structure served a dual purpose, she had to enter on the days they squeezed sugar cane.

With a stick in his hand, little Santiago drove the large animal around the circular perimeter of the men's house. This motion activated the large central roller that was placed vertically in the middle of the *trapiche,* while wooden cogs activated the other two rollers on either side. Malgalita fed the long stalks of cut cane between the rollers, and the extracted juice ran down into a wooden trough, then into a large, heavy, iron caldron.

As Santiago gloomily drove the huge *buey* around the circle, he thought of Sama. She had been his first playmate, his full sister, daughter of his unknown mother. His sense of loss was great. What would old Maldia do now? She would be left alone with the baby. How he wished he could return to her hut. Here he was not learning much about Kogi manhood. Huilde rarely spoke to him, and he was always left to guard the farm even on the rare occasions that Malgalita went to the village site to spend the night in a little round women's house.

Kogi child driving the donkey that turns the trapiche to squeeze out the sugar cane juice.

The squeezing of the sugar cane was now finished. Santiago helped Malgalita carry the heavy caldron to the fire where they supported it on three carefully placed rocks. Malgalita would stir it with a large, wooden ladle with holes in the bowl, lifting it high in the air, the liquid sugar returning to the caldron through the holes. In this way she kept the huge pot from boiling over until the sweet syrup reached the "hard-ball-stage." Then it was scooped with wooden paddles into rectangular molds also made of wood. The next morning the cool rectangular blocks would be hung in an old *gama* or stacked on a special shelf in the smoke of the fire to discourage the cockroaches where it would be ready for household use or for sale to other families who did not have a *trapiche*.

Santiago returned the white ox to its pasture and sat down on the edge of an outcropping rock, staring down the valley. How he longed to see the world beyond those mountains and learn the *muldigabba*. Would his opportunity never come?

Early one morning about a week later, Maldia appeared at the doorway of Huilde's men's house. Baby Samanu shared her back with a large jute *gama*. Her face was sad and drawn. "Come with me, " she ordered without ceremony. "We are going to my brother, *Dakua*, in Santa Rosa."

Obediently Santiago grabbed his one extra garment from under the roof, picked up his machete, and followed without comment. For several days they trudged through the mountains taking turns with the bundle and the baby, who though small and thin for his age, was still a heavy burden for the old woman

Santiago

and young boy. As they traveled they sustained themselves on green plantains that Maldia had dried on the roof of her house in preparation for the trip, and chunks of *panela*. At last the trail broke out over a pass, and Santiago could gaze for many miles upon a panoramic view of the mountains, which stirred his blood and reawakened his desire for adventure and knowledge of the Kogi myths and traditions.

Santiago and Maldia lived with relatives in Santa Rosa for several years, but there was never much opportunity for him, a virtual orphan boy except for his *haba weizhu* (old grandmother), to learn much of the Kogi *muldigabba*. All the *mamas* and older men with a reputation for knowledge of the Kogi traditions had a number of acolytes and young relatives with more claims to their attentions than an unknown orphan boy from a distant village with no one but an elderly woman to recommend him.

On one of the eastern slopes of the Sierra, lies a village known as *Pueblo Viejo* (The Old Town). It has been there for years and is composed of Spanish speaking people who make their living as middlemen, buying products from the Indians and selling them at a profit in the market towns in the valley. On the eastern side of the mountains, the Malayos and Kogis live in close proximity to one another and even rub shoulders with the Arhuacos who have migrated up from the south. The Kogis as a rule live higher up the slopes and have fewer contacts with the Spanish speakers than do the other two tribes.

After living in Santa Rosa for a number of years, Santiago was taken by his grandmother to actually live in the town of Pueblo Viejo. They resided with a named Jhon-Jhon. This experience brought Santiago no nearer to his dream of learning the Kogi *muldigabba,* but it did open up a new vista of learning to him, as he began to pick up the Spanish language.

After living in *Pueblo Viejo* for a year, they returned to the village of Palomino. Maldia was still the owner of the farm there where Huilde lived, but they only stayed a few weeks, as one of the great opportunities of Santiago's life presented itself.

Mama Julian, mentor of Santiago, and great grandfather
to most of the current Kogi Christians.

Kogi men do not shake hands, they exchange coca.

Chapter 12

A Dream Realized

An older daughter of Maldia, who had left home so long ago as to have been presumed dead and more than half forgotten, appeared on the scene. Miracle of miracles to young Santiago, this now middle-aged woman was the wife of Mama Julian, one of the famous *mamas* of his generation. The obligation of a son-in-law is life long. Even after the period of bride service is ended, and he can take his wife away to his own land and family, he is always on call to serve his mother-in-law and father-in-law. If he can be located, he must come to their aid. Now Mama Julian, important man though he was, must respond to his obligations. Maldia, Santiago, and Samanu went to live with him.

Now, for the first time in his life, Santiago's boyhood dream was realized. He had become a part of the household of a learned *Mama*. He had a chance to learn the *muldigabba*. It was not an excellent chance to be sure, but still a chance. As a boy of around 13 or 14, he shared the men's house with all the male members of the *mama's* household. Although he was a mere *nashi*, a person without importance, inheritance, nor position, he was alert to take advantage of every opportunity to learn.

Sometimes Mama Julian had visitors, important men from other villages. All night long they would lie in their hammocks in the men's house, chewing their coca and scraping their sticks against their lime filled gourds. On these occasions Santiago's eyes never closed. He lay awake in the darkness, his intense desire to learn the *muldigabba* stimulating him and keeping drowsiness away as effectively as the coca drug did for the older men. On the nights of the biweekly reunion, he was alert to be present in the large men's council house at the village, his eyes wide open and his mind alert, an anxious look on his face as he wrinkled up his forehead in his effort to absorb and retain all that was said. He wanted to remember all of the *muldigabba*. He would not let one word fall on the ground and be lost.

Mama Julian had a son named Miguel, a boy just a little bit younger than Santiago. Miguel was being trained to replace his father as *mama* someday, but although he had been trained from infancy, Miguel lacked the desire to learn that burned in Santiago. The newcomer managed to be present as much as possible when the old *mama* was teaching his son. Soon Santiago's knowledge of Kogi lore surpassed that of Miguel.

Mama Julian appreciated the interest of his new pupil and took special pains with him. Ever after, Santiago would speak of Mama Julian as "the one who raised me," or "the one who was like a father to me," but he had nothing but disdain for Miguel, "the one who had every opportunity but didn't bother to learn."

Living with the family of Mama Julian, Santiago also began to fulfill his desire to travel and see more of the Kogi area. They went first to the large village of Don Diego to the north, then crossing the 'gexa' (land above the tree line) to the west came at last to the Kogi village of San Andres on the western slopes of the Sierra.

But now a new interest had developed in Santiago. His contact with the non-Kogis Spanish speaking man in *Pueblo Viejo* had whetted his appetite to learn the Spanish language and the way of life of the non-Indian people. He spent some months living with a man called Old Benito and learning Spanish.

During these years Santiago reached his full height of four and a half feet. The scarcity of protein and other nutrients in his early youth had stunted his growth. He would always be a miniature of the man he could have been, but he had survived. He had been a "good seed". His body had learned to adapt to the available diet. He was strong and resilient. He could out-work and out-lift a much larger man. No one knew nor cared to know his chronological age. He was declared to be full-grown and was initiated into manhood by his mentor, Mama Julian.

Santiago & Gloria.

Now, some 20 years later, Santiago was seated across the table from me in our small kitchen in the little mud house he had built for us on his farm. He had placed his ever present *sugi* (poporo), a long necked hollow gourd containing lime to activate the dried coca lives that he carried in a small pouch, into his red and white striped *sugame* (cotton carrying bag). He was the most outgoing Kogi we had met. To him we were his own private missionaries. He tried to be very helpful, answering our questions about his life and culture. I had already taken notes on the details he had given me about his early life and childhood. Now he was prepared to tape-record the remainder of his life story.

"After I was initiated, I married a woman named Alicia," Santiago continues his story. (She seems to have been a *nashi*, a person without means or importance, perhaps a widow or an orphan or both, as no bride service was mentioned.) "About that time I started making trips to Santa Marta and Barranquilla. I went to the *gexa* (high mountain country above the tree line) and gathered herbs of medicinal value. Then I took them to town and sold them. This way I made a few pesos. I was the only one who did this. This was the first time I had money. I bought a blanket. I was very poor in those days. I had nothing.

Maldia (Santiago and Alicia's daughter) Santiago and Alfonso.

"Then I went to work for Simon (a mama who later befriended us) in Don Diego. He had a big sugar cane field. I worked for him every day. I squeezed sugar cane. This was when *panela* was cheap, 20 blocks for a peso. (In 1983 one block of panela cost 15 pesos.) I worked this way for a long time together with Alicia. I bought a cow and sold it.

"After one more year, Simon sold his sugar cane field. Then I started a little farm of my own, and I planted a few *platano* trees.

"After that I made a little farm near the stream of *Pico Raton*. Then I bought a sugar cane farm from Benito. I bought it for 50 pesos. I did very well, and soon I didn't lack anything. After that I sold that farm for 500 pesos. Then I came to this side (the western side) and bought a farm. It had *platano* trees, and I planted sugar cane. I had a *trapiche* built. Alfonso's father built it for me. (Alfonso was our young language helper.) I paid 50 pesos. Every day I was squeezing sugar cane.

"Then the white people started to buy land. They told me the land wasn't mine. It was the government's land. 'We are receiving this land,' they said, so I sold it for 900 pesos. So I made another farm and had another *trapiche* built. This time it cost me 100 pesos. A man from Mamarongo made it for me. I was here, (near San Javier) living with the woman who I had, Alicia, but she left me.

"Then I married Isabel, Alfonso's sister. I lived with her in Don Diego two or three years (doing bride service). I was happy with this woman.

"After that I came here again (San Javier). She lived with me here. After about five months, we went back to Don Diego and stayed there about ten months working for my father-in-law. My farm went to wrack and ruin. Everything died. I came back again and fixed up my farm. Then we went back to Don Diego again but only stayed a short time. We returned to San Javier and stayed here.

"After that Isabel died. She went fishing after a heavy rain. She slipped on the rocks and drowned in the river. I was very sad. I didn't know what to do. I didn't feel like eating because I loved her very much. We were happy together. She died, and I was grieving. I was all alone. The other Indians didn't care about me; they didn't help me at all.

I have had six children. All of them died except one named Maldia. She lives in Don Diego with Alicia. They died of pneumonia and diarrhea. Alicia had four that died. Isabel only had one, but it died too.

"Then Maria Elena came to live with me. We were living together here when you came."

Santiago and Maria Elena
transport supplies with their ox.

María Elena with her baby, Margot

Chapter 13

Maria Elena's Story

Santiago's Farm,
La Sierra Nevada de Santa Marta
1966

I was sitting with Maria Elena, Santiago's wife, on the lean-to porch of our mud house perched on a flattened ridge across the river from the colonist settlement of San Javier. Finding no level land on which to build us a house, Santiago had dug off the rounded edge of the slope rising behind his own small home of split cane and thatch. Maria Elena nestled into the green and white plastic webbed lawn chair, holding the microphone of the tape recorder with her right hand. With her left hand she signaled that she was ready to begin taping her life story.

"At first I lived well with my parents. Then after I got older, I didn't live well anymore." A cloud passed over Maria Elena's round brown face. Her lovely dark, luminous eyes filled with sorrow as her mind reached back into the past. "My father was kind to me until the bat visited me." (The bat is a Kogi euphemism for the menses. A visit from a vampire bat would explain bloodstains.) Lowering her voice, she continued in a whisper, "You know what that means. We say it that way so the children won't understand. Now, after the bat visited me, my father changed. He brought a man home to work on the farm. 'Talk with him! Talk with him! ' my father told me. But I ran away; I hid in the jungle. I slept in the grass. (Talk is a Kogi euphemism for sexual relations.)

"My father searched until he found me. He hit me! He hit me hard! He kept hitting me! All the way home he hit me! 'Talk with him!' my father said. I talked with him. At first I didn't want to, then it wasn't so bad, then I liked to talk with him. Just when I was liking him very much, my father sent him away. 'He doesn't work hard enough,' he told me.

"Soon my father came home with another man. This one was very ugly. I did not want to talk with him. 'Talk with him!' said my father. 'You must talk with him very well. He is a good worker.'

"Soon this man also left. Another one came, and another one. Sometimes they left because my father made them work so hard. Sometimes they wanted me to run away with them. Some wanted to stay, but after they had been there awhile, my father made them go away. He did not want me to go with them. He did not want to lose me. He always wanted to have a son-in-law working for him. One of his hands had been mangled by a *trapiche*, so he only had one arm. He wanted to always have a new son-in-law working for him.

Inocencio

"One day I decided to leave with the man who was my husband. We went to his father's house in Pueblo Viejo. We were there awhile, and then my husband left me. He really left me; I was all alone! I went back to my father. Then Inocencio (a Kogi neighbor whom I knew) came to my father's house. He was an old man. 'Make me a *trapiche*,' my father told him. I thought he was just there to make a *trapiche*. I can never talk with him, I thought. But as always before, my father made me talk with him. If I don't talk with him, I will have to live alone out in the jungle, I thought.

"I thought and thought. It seemed very distasteful to me to talk with him. 'Talk with him,' my father ordered. I began to talk with him; I talked with him. Very well I began to talk with him.

"Then my mother became jealous of me. She thought my father, himself, wanted to talk with me. 'Leave with Inocencio,' my parents ordered me. I thought and thought. I returned to Pueblo Viejo. I was there when Inocencio came. I went down to the plain with him. To Dibulla (a Colombian town on the north coast) we went.

"One day my mother arrived. She was looking for my father. She was very jealous of me. Later when I went to look for bananas, she found me. 'I'm going to hit you,' she said, and she hit me on the head with a machete. My head was cut open, and the blood was running down. I ran away. I ran to where the non-Indian people live. I ran to the house of a man named Janicu. I complained to him, and he got a court order against my mother.

"Why did this happen? I thought. Before, when I was young, I didn't talk with men. Here, once more I am happy. Why all this trouble with men? Why talk with them? This is what I was thinking.

"One night I decided to leave. I thought of going home. I started on the trail to my house. Up, up, up I went. But then I thought, my father is expecting me

Maria Elena

to return soon so he can get another son-in-law. I won't go back to my father, at least not very soon. I kept climbing. Night came, and then another one. I passed the town of Santa Rosa. I slept under a high rock. While it was still dark, I got up and kept going. Late that day I arrived at Palomino. My grandfather lived there. 'Whose fault is it that you are here?' he asked me.

"'It's my mother's fault that I am here,' I said. 'My mother is very jealous of me. She told me to get out. She told me there were many pigs and cows here. She sent me here,' I lied. 'Later there will come a request to let me stay here, if it is all right with you.'

"'Your mother won't gain anything out of this,' grumbled my grandfather. He would not let me stay. I slept that night, and the next day I hurt my foot. It hurt very much, and I couldn't leave. I stayed and washed my foot with warm water. When it was a little better, I left.

"I walked for days. I walked through here (the area around San Javier). I continued to Don Diego, and so I lived in Don Diego. Inocencio was there. I had a baby. I named her Tomasa after my younger sister.

Tomasa and her friend, Patricia

"In Don Diego, the people drink a lot of rum and become very drunk. Inocencio got drunk and became very angry. He hit me. Why did he hit me? I thought. I haven't done anything wrong. I planned to leave, but then he came and talked nicely to me, and I didn't leave. But later I did leave, taking Tomasa with me. I was expecting another baby. I went to the house of Simon. (The mama who later befriended us.) I was like a widow.

"Inocencio came looking for me. I talked with him again, and then all the people got drunk, and I did too. I was in a house with several men. We were all drunk, and the door was closed. I began to feel very sad. Why did I do this? I thought. We were just back together again and happy.

"Inocencio was very angry. He went and saw the commissioner (the civil authority). We all had to go down to the plain, and they fined me. While we were down in the plain my labor started, and so they took me to the hospital in Cienega. I was very frightened. When no one was watching me, I ran away. I started back up into the mountains. My baby, Cecilia, was born beside the road.

Inocencio with Margarita, the wife he traded his oldest daughter for after he left Maria Elena. The children are Cecilia, Tomasa, Patricia and baby Losalba.

"I came to San Pedro. (After the Kogi village of San Andres was taken over by non-Indian people, it was renamed San Pedro.) Then we went up into the high mountain country. It was very cold. It was raining. I couldn't walk well. 'We'll go back to San Pedro,' said Inocencio.

"I thought we would never arrive. How many hours will it take, I wondered. I was very cold. There was little sun. We arrived in the rain, completely soaked. Then we stayed in San Pedro. After awhile Inocencio left me. I continued in San Pedro, living there with the white inspector, talking with the inspector.

"Then I went to live with other Indians. I was like a widow. Inocencio came and took my two children. He traded his teen-aged daughter for another wife and bought a farm near San Javier. Santiago's wife had died. He was all alone. He was very lonely. I came here to live with him. He went to the inspector at San Pedro, and they made Inocencio give Cecilia back to me. Tomasa stayed with Inocencio."

Just then five-year-old Cecilia came running up from Maria Elena's house. The baby, Margot, had awakened. Maria Elena slowly set down her empty coffee cup and reluctantly left the comfort of the folding lawn chair. Her story was told. She padded on bare feet down the hill to care for her baby.

Soon she emerged from her house. The baby was in her *busu* on her mother's back along with a large jute *gama* swinging from a head strap. In the *gama* was a gallon and a half metal milk pail. Behind her came Cecilia with a smaller *gama* containing a long necked gourd. Machete in hand as a precaution against snakes, Maria Elena and her daughter started off down the steep path to the river to bring back the next day's supply of water.

Cecilia, 5 years & Gloria, 2 years

As I watched little Cecilia trudge down the trail behind her mother my heart was saddened. Will Cecilia's life be a repetition of her mother's sad story? I wondered. Surely it will be better because we have come.

A Minnesota Mom moves to Colombia, South America on January 3, 1964

Books in this series written by
Patricia Carlson Stendal

Minnesota Mom in the Land of the Ancient Mother

For more information: patstendal@aol.com

Website: www.colombiaparacristo.com

Books written by the Stendal Family

High Adventure in Colombia
   by Chad Stendal

The Guerrillas Have Taken Our Son
   by Chad & Pat Stendal

Walking In The Spirit
   by Chadwick Martin Stendal

40 Years in Colombia
Lomalinda: There and Back Again
   by Patricia & Gloria Stendal

This Gospel of the Kingdom
   by Chad Stendal

Are Millions of Christians Really Safe?
   by Chad Stendal

The Problem Christ Came to Solve
   by Chad Stendal

Rescue The Captors
   by Russell Stendal

The Beatitudes: God's Plan For Battle
   by Russell Stendal

The Tabernacle of David
   by Russell Stendal

The Elijah Who Is To Come
   by Russell Stendal

...And The Earth Shall Respond To The Wheat...
   by Russell Stendal

TO ORDER ANY OF THE THESE BOOKS

Ordering books in the USA:

Dwight Clough
1223 West Main Street #228
Sun Prairie, WI 53590

books@dwightclough.com
http://www.dwightclough.com/

PARA PEDIR ALGUNO DE ESTOS LIBROS

Librería en Colombia:

Colombia Para Cristo
Calle 44 #13-69 Local 1
Bogotá, Colombia
Tel: (571) 346-1419 * 338-3807

Email: libreria@fuerzadepaz.com
www.fuerzadepaz.com

Afterward

The stories in Chapter 5 & 6, were told to me by my mother, Eva Carlson. Before her death at 89 years in 1986, she read and approved these chapters. More of my early family life will be told in Volume II.

The stories in Chapter 7, were told by my mother-in-law, Jean Stendal. Jean passed away in 1987 at 87 years of age. She and her husband, Russell, will also appear again in Volume II.

Chapters 8 – 12 were told by Santiago Dingula when we lived on his farm 1965 – 1973. Volume IV will be mostly about our life on his farm. Santiago and Maria Elena will also appear briefly in Volume V.

The Stendal's work with the Kogis is an ongoing ministry, currently motivated by the Kogis themselves, since we are unable to go visit them due to the political unrest of the Sierra, they come to us when they want to see us.

Many of the Children & Grandchildren of the people mentioned in these 6 volumes are now in the valley of decision. They must be given the dignity of being allowed to choose for themselves, that right belongs to every human being.